THE BEGINNER'S GUIDE TO MANGA AND ANIME

マンガ・アニメ入門

LEARN THE HISTORY
EXPLORE THE ART
MEET THE CREATORS

SHUICHIRO TAKEDA

武田 秀一郎

SCHOLASTIC INC.

ISBN 978-1-338-89337-3

10 9 8 7 6 5 4 3 2   24 25 26 27 28

Printed in the U.S.A.   40
First printing 2024

Book design by Tim Palin Creative

Photos ©: 2: The Yomiuri Shimbun via AP Images; 3: ton koene/Alamy Stock Photo; 3 background and throughout: burao_sato/Shutterstock; 4: limonene_ita/Shutterstock; 12-13 top: Historic Collection/Alamy Stock Photo; 12-13 bottom: The Picture Art Collection/Alamy Stock Photo; 14 left: Library of Congress; 14 right: Smithsonian Libraries; 15 top left and center: Library of Congress; 15 top right: Arthur Tress Collection of Japanese Illustrated Books/ University of Pennsylvania; 15 bottom left: CPA Media Pte Ltd/Alamy Stock Photo; 15 bottom right: Peter Hermes Furian/Alamy Stock Photo; 16 left: National Portrait Gallery/Smithsonian Institution; 16 right: Rapp Halour/Alamy Stock Photo; 17 left: duncan1890/DigitalVision Vectors/Getty Images; 17 right: Zuri Swimmer/Alamy Stock Photo; 18-19 top: The New York Public Library; 18 bottom left: George Rinhart/Corbis via Getty Images; 22 bottom: The Asahi Shimbun via Getty Images; 28 bottom right: TOSHIFUMI KITAMURA/AFP via Getty Images; 41 bottom: 600dpi; 48: dodotone/Shutterstock; 72: The Yomiuri Shimbun via AP Images; 80: kuremo/Shutterstock; 92 top: Photo 12/Alamy Stock Photo; 92 bottom: Photo 12/Alamy Stock Photo; 93: Photo 12/Alamy Stock Photo; 94: BFA/Alamy Stock Photo; 95 top left: Mary Evans Picture Library Ltd/Alamy Stock Photo; 95 top right: Everett Collection, Inc./Alamy Stock Photo; 95 bottom right: Album/Alamy Stock Photo; 97: Photo 12/Alamy Stock Photo; 98 left: Album/Alamy Stock Photo; 98 right: Photo 12/Alamy Stock Photo; 99: Photo 12/Alamy Stock Photo; 100 top: Aflo Co. Ltd./Alamy Stock Photo; 100 bottom: Panther Media GmbH/Alamy Stock Photo; 101: BFA/Alamy Stock Photo; 104-105: Album/Alamy Stock Photo; 106: World Discovery/Alamy Stock Photo; 107: Aflo/Shutterstock; 109 top: Trevor Mogg/Alamy Stock Photo; 109 bottom: Japan travel photography/Alamy Stock Photo; 110: Kabuki photo © SHOCHIKU; 114: Maximum Film/Alamy Stock Photo; 115 bottom: Kyodo News Stills via Getty Images.

THIS PROJECT WAS A LABOR OF LOVE.

I WOULD LIKE TO EXPRESS MY DEEPEST GRATITUDE TO GEORGE LEONIDOU OF SCHOLASTIC FOR BRINGING THIS OPPORTUNITY TO ME AND TO ROBERT CORY FOR BELIEVING IN ME AND CONTINUING TO SUPPORT ME IN EVERY WAY. I AM ALSO GRATEFUL TO MY PARENTS IN JAPAN, WHO HAVE ALWAYS ENCOURAGED ME TO PURSUE MY DREAMS.

—SHUICHIRO TAKEDA

It took a village to create this book! Scholastic gratefully recognizes the cooperation of Bandai Namco, Josh Bettinger, Jessie Bowman, Aerin Csigay, Mark de Vera, Priscilla Eakeley, Crystal Erickson, Fantagraphics, Jael Fogle, Froebel-Kan Co., Ltd., Fujiko F. Fujio Pro, Yuriko Fukazawa, Gordon W. Prange Collection, University of Maryland, Donna Grosso, Conrad Groth, Maki Hakui, Hanavbara, Sayumi Hasegawa, Kaori Hirose, Hiromi Kadowaki, Charles King, Alexis Kirsch, Erik Ko, Kobayashi-san of the Tokiwa-sō Manga Museum, Sayaka Kuroda, Last Gasp, Yaffa Jaskoll, Amy Levenson, Jennifer Liu, the family of Katsuji Matsumoto, Kohei Miyamoto, Hideko Mizuno, Mari Morimoto, DVM, Mukai-san, the National Film Archive of Japan, Cian O'Day, Yukari Ortlieb, Kristin Parcell, the Pokémon Company, Jennifer Rinaldi, Masako Sakano, Kayo Sekizawa, Seven Seas Entertainment, Megumi Shimada, Shin-Ei Animation Co., Ltd., Shogakukan, Shueisha, Jake Snyder, Cheung Tai, Yasue Takada, Macoto Takahashi, Rumiko Takahashi, Takayoshi Takahashi, Natsuki Takaya, Emily Teresa, Tezuka Productions, Toho Co., Ltd., Colin Turner, UDON Entertainment, Yui Uemura, Michie Utsuhara, VIZ Media, Yen Press, and Lizzy Yoder.

Scholastic also gratefully acknowledges the expert content review of this book by Dr. Andrea Horbinski.

Without them, this book would be a shadow of what it currently is. Thank you!

CONTENTS

ANIME

INTRODUCTION
はじめに

DEAR READER,

Welcome to the amazing world of manga and anime! Depending on your interests, there is an endless selection of genres to choose from. From *Dragon Ball* to *Naruto*, *Sailor Moon* to *Pokémon*, the stories and gifted creators of manga and anime offer up fascinating worlds populated with engaging characters. Simply put, there are manga and anime out there for everyone, including you!

Japanese comics are called *manga*. They are a printed form of media (now also digital), usually in black and white, that encourages you to use your imagination. As you glance from page to page, you can add your own voices and colors to the characters and enhance the stories with new ideas that pop up in your mind. For example, you may imagine a shy girl character with a soft-spoken voice or a cheeky boy talking in a loud excited tone. You can also read and experience manga at your own pace; some days you may want to dwell on a few captivating panels for several minutes, and at other times you may swiftly fly through the pages. You can enjoy manga whenever you want, as much as you want, and at whatever pace you want. Your imagination will conjure up color, sound, and movement all at the same time; it really is pure entertainment!

The word *anime* refers to Japanese cartoons. Unlike manga, anime uses color, sound, and movement to enhance the story line and influence how you experience the characters, atmosphere, and mood. Colors may highlight changes in the characters' facial expressions, sound gives voice to the characters and scenery such as the blowing of the wind, and movement generates action in the scene. For example, villains may have dark color palettes and deep voices to show how menacing they are. In contrast, cheerful heroes may appear in vibrant colors and have lively expressions. When they engage in battle, the sound effects, background music, and movement combine to show how important the fight is.

Nowadays, we can learn, explore, and admire the lives, cultures, and thoughts of people who differ from us. The same goes for manga and anime; manga and anime are filled with situations we cannot experience in our everyday lives and ideas we would never think of as our own. You may come across a manga or anime that nourishes your mind and transforms your life. Fate and destiny are critical elements in manga and anime stories, as they may be in your own life.

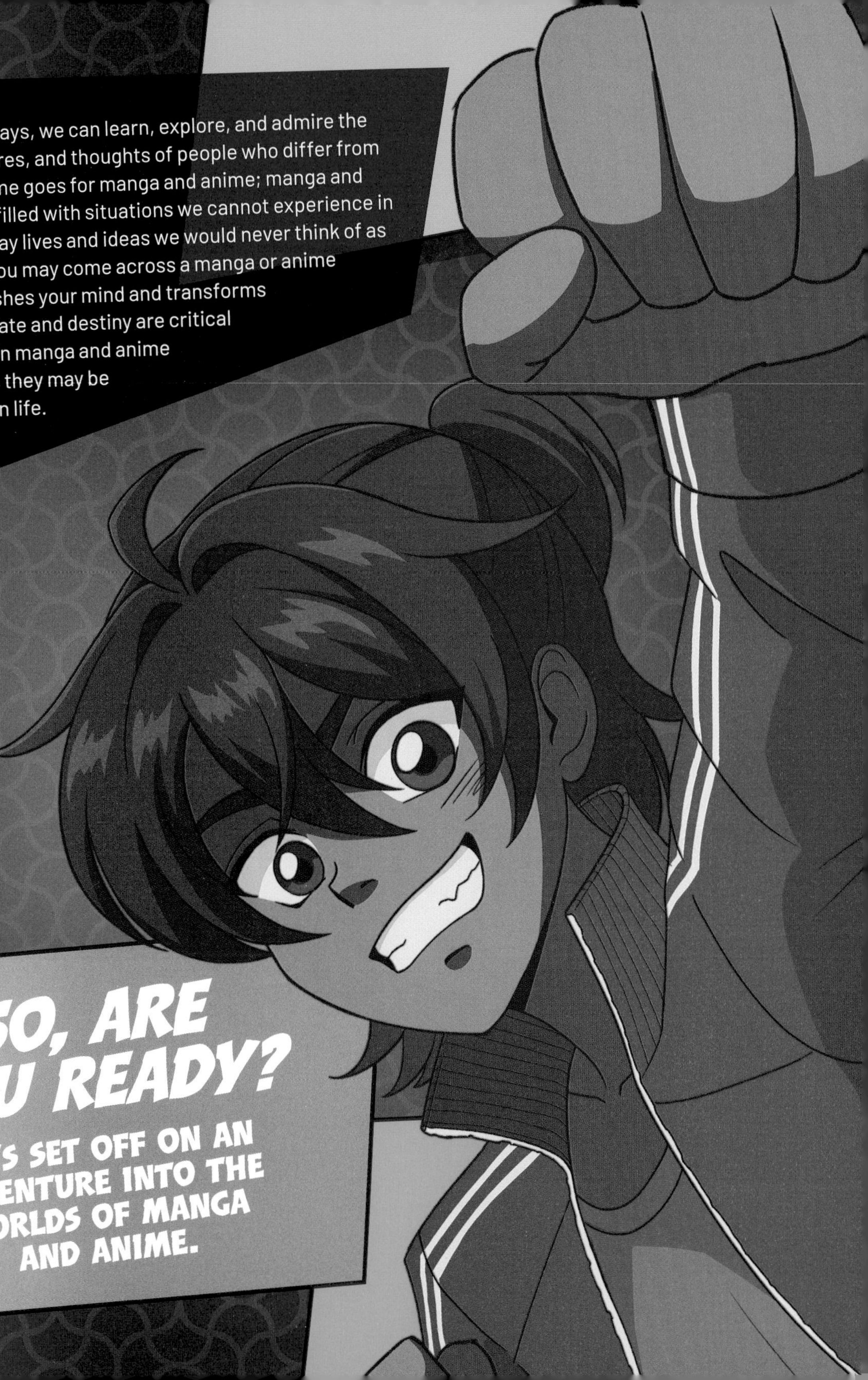

SO, ARE YOU READY?

LET'S SET OFF ON AN ADVENTURE INTO THE WORLDS OF MANGA AND ANIME.

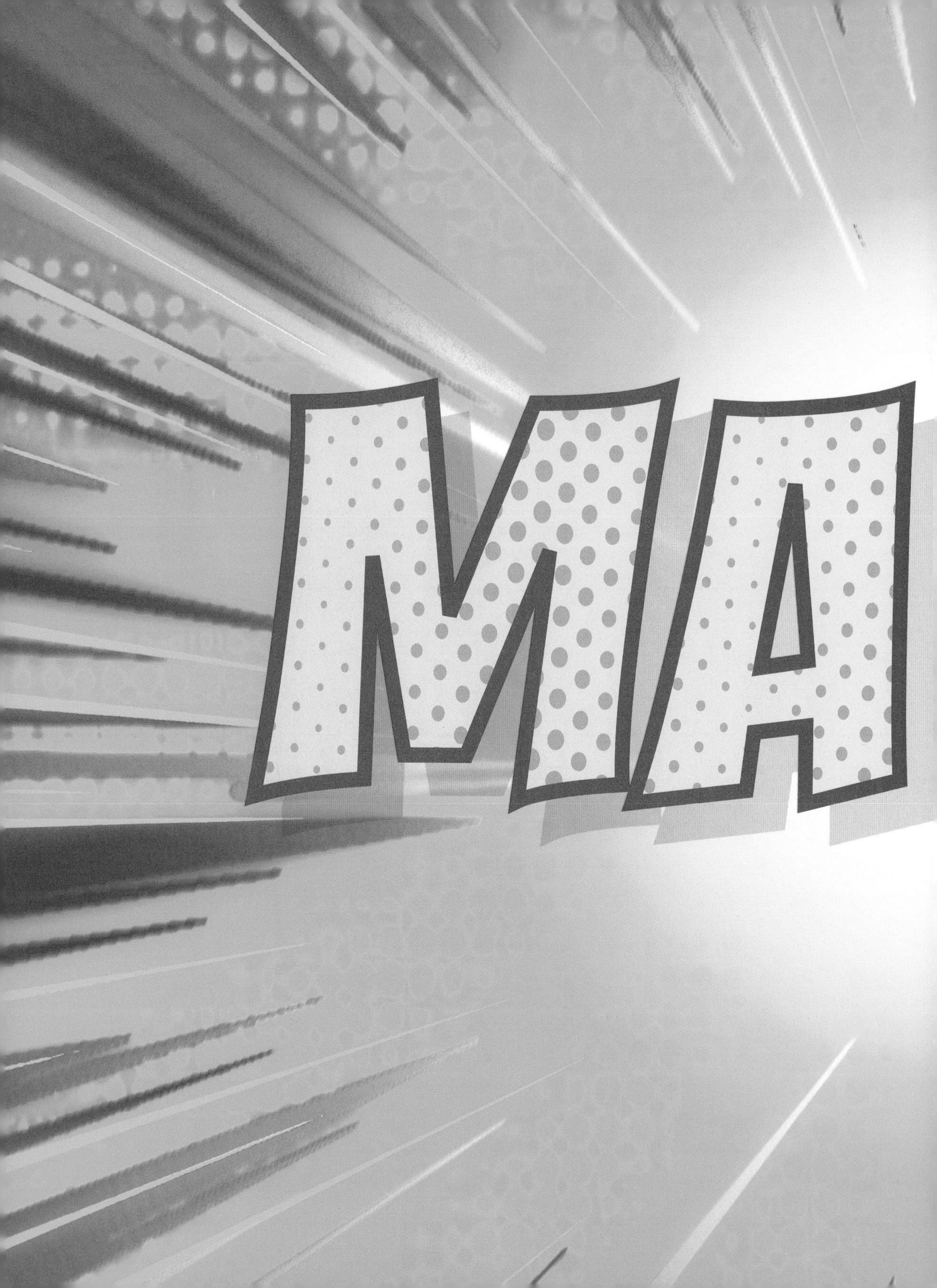
MA

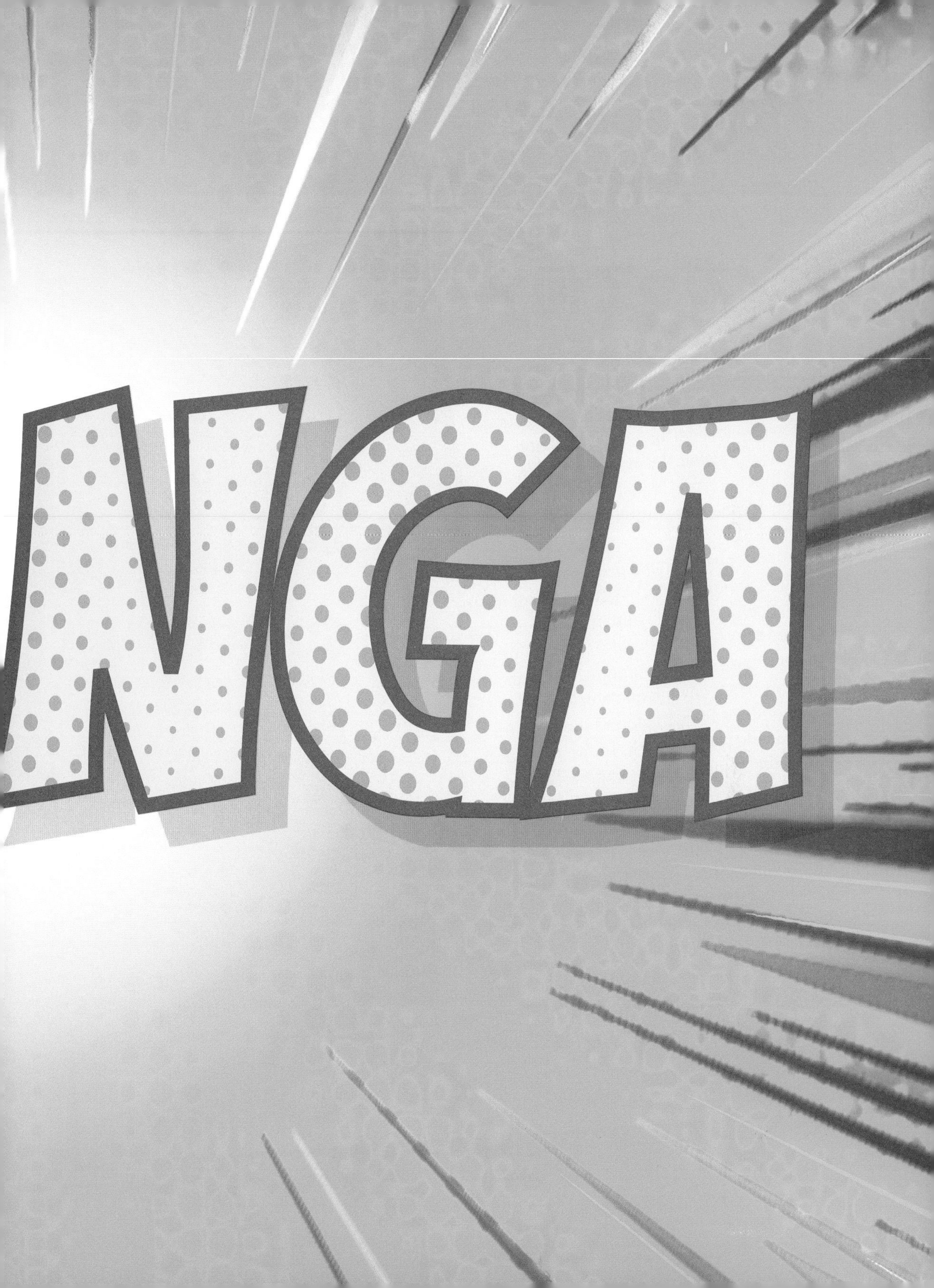
NGA

THE DEFINITION OF MANGA

マンガって何？

The word *manga* is composed of two Japanese sounds and is used worldwide to refer to Japanese comics. The sound *man* means "whimsical" or "humorous," and *ga* refers to a "drawing." So *manga* refers to drawings that entertain readers—but not necessarily for the sole purpose of making them laugh.

Over time, talented *manga-ka*, or manga artists, have created a wide variety of genres to appeal to children and adults alike. In Japan, action, sports, romance, and manga dealing with family, work, and social issues can easily be purchased at bookstores, train stations, and convenience stores. You will often see adults reading manga as they commute by train back and forth to work. Today, more and more people read manga on their smartphones and tablets. On what device do you read manga?

There are several styles of manga. The first and most basic are one-frame manga (*hito-koma manga*). These are single pictures with a funny or satirical message and are drawn with exaggerated brushstrokes that invite laughter. In the opinion pages of newspapers, you may have noticed single-frame political cartoons containing caricatures of well-known figures. They easily convey the artist's opinion so that readers can readily understand them. There are also four-frame manga (*yon-koma manga*) and story manga, the style that may come to mind when you hear the word *manga*. Both these styles easily follow a story line.

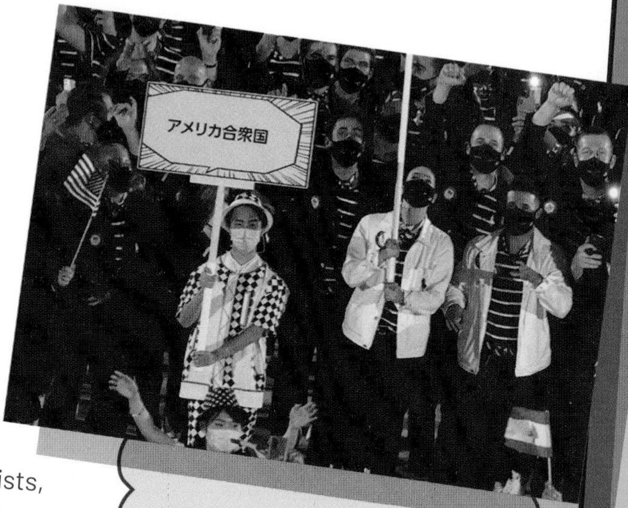

アメリカ合衆国

SO SUGOI!

During the Opening Ceremony of the Tokyo Olympics in 2021, the entrance of the athletes drew much attention. The background music was from video games, and the signs introducing the countries employed the traditional manga techniques of *fukidashi* and *kōka-sen*.

SO SUGOI!

There are three Manga Day anniversaries in Japan! Two of these honor the greatest *manga-ka*, Osamu Tezuka, also known as the "God of Manga."

FEBRUARY 9

This date was chosen by Mandarake, a chain of secondhand stores specializing in anime, manga, and related items, to commemorate the anniversary of Osamu Tezuka's death in 1989.

JULY 17

The choice of this day does not come from Japanese manga but instead from Great Britain. On July 17, 1841, the British illustrated weekly magazine *Punch* was first published. The magazine's style is considered an inspiration for manga culture, so the date has been designated as another Manga Day.

NOVEMBER 3

Culture Day is an official Japanese holiday dedicated to the appreciation of Japanese culture and arts. It also happens to be the birthday of Osamu Tezuka! For that reason, the Japan Cartoonists Association chose Culture Day as one of the Manga Days.

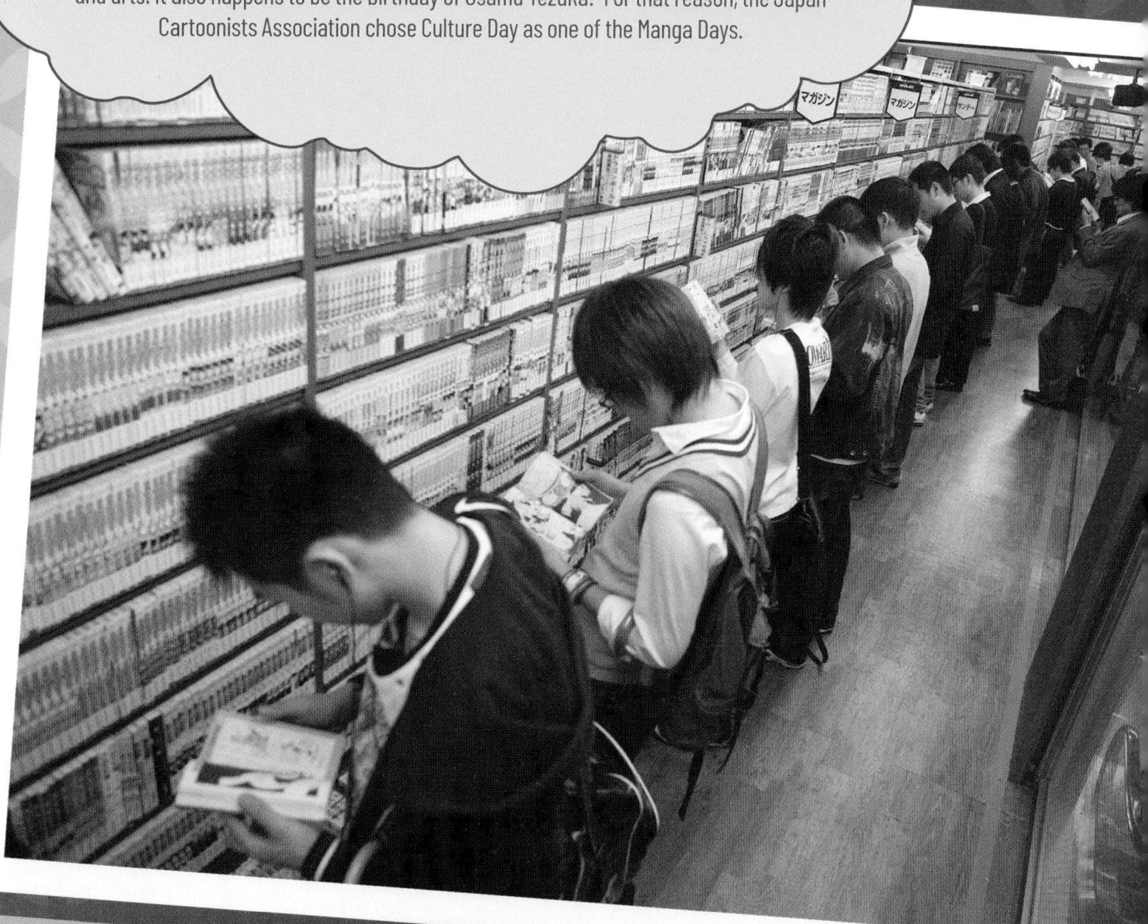
マガジン
マガジン
サンデー

HOW TO READ MANGA AND MANGA TECHNIQUES

Manga are read "top to bottom" and "right to left." In the past, each manga panel was numbered to help readers follow them in the correct order.

Some prominent features of manga include:

FUKIDASHI (SPEECH BALLOONS)

Fukidashi are speech bubbles that reveal dialogue and vary in appearance depending on whether characters are shouting out loud or thinking. For example, solid, circular *fukidashi* can express normal speech, while a cloudlike design can represent inner thoughts.

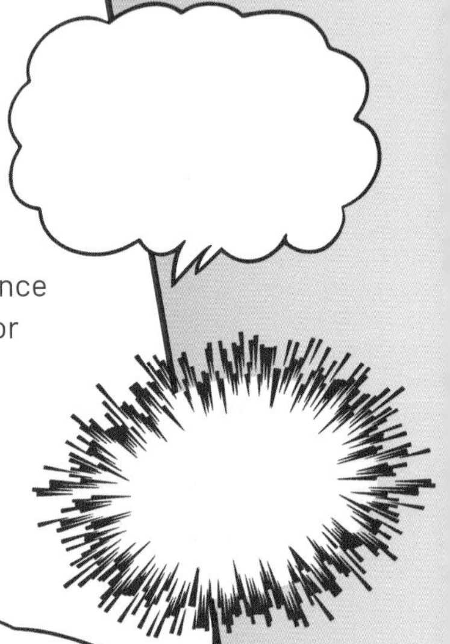

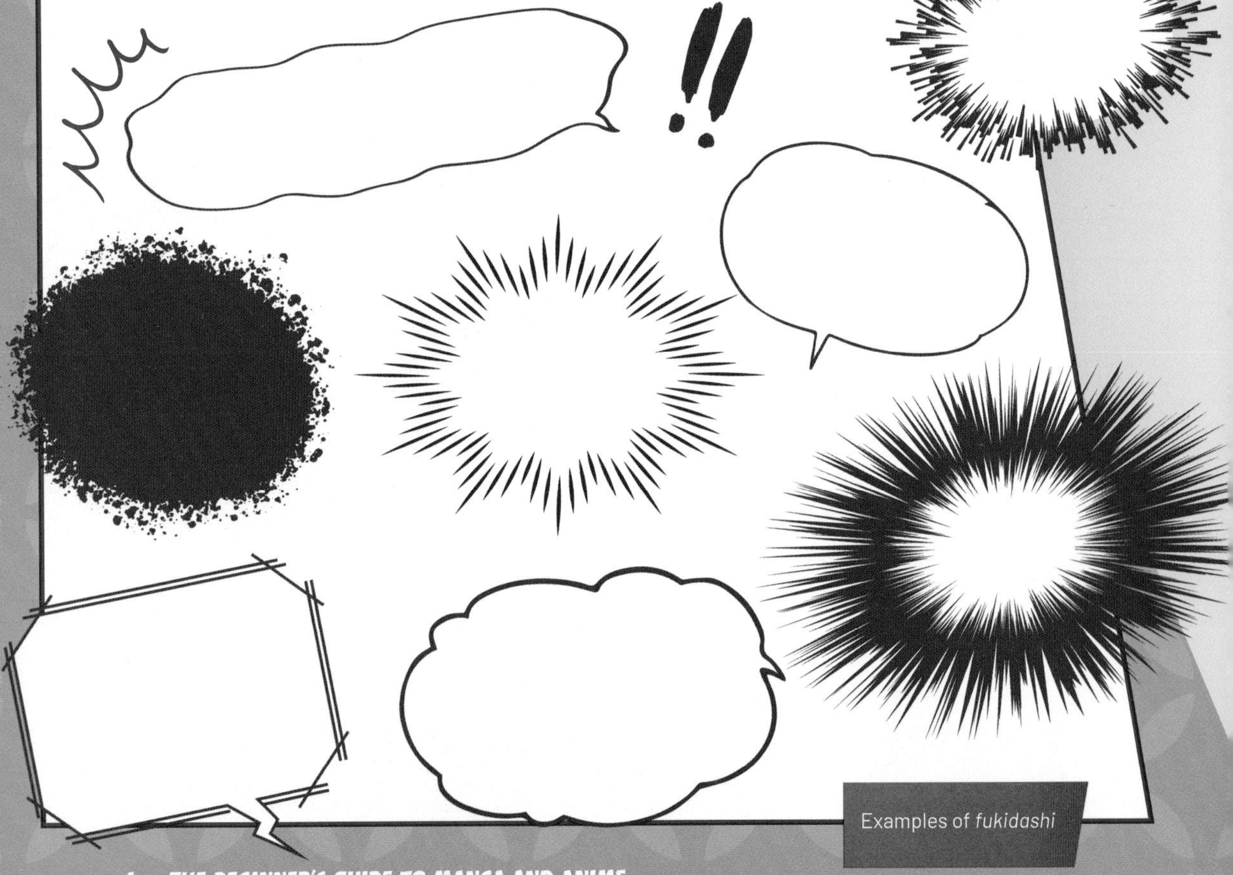

Examples of *fukidashi*

ONOMATOPOEIA

Japanese is a language rich in onomatopoeia—words that mimic actual sounds or directly represent human emotions and objects. For example, *zaa-zaa* indicates the sound of pouring rain, *waku-waku* expresses the excitement one feels due to a pleasant experience, and *kira-kira* calls to mind twinkling stars.

In manga, onomatopoeia is written in specific ways to convey tone, such as small, thin characters to depict quiet scenes and large, bold characters for loud sounds and intense emotions. Onomatopoeia supplies the subtle details of emotion and movement that enliven otherwise static drawings.

Example of onomatopoeia in *Dragon Ball*, courtesy of VIZ Media

DRAGON BALL © 1984 by BIRD STUDIO/ SHUEISHA Inc.

SO SUGOI!

Pikachu is one of the most recognizable characters in pop culture, but did you know Pikachu's name derives from two Japanese onomatopoeia? *Pika-pika* indicates a spark of lightning and *chuu* is the sound squeaking mice make, so it makes perfect sense that Pikachu is an electric-type Mouse Pokémon!

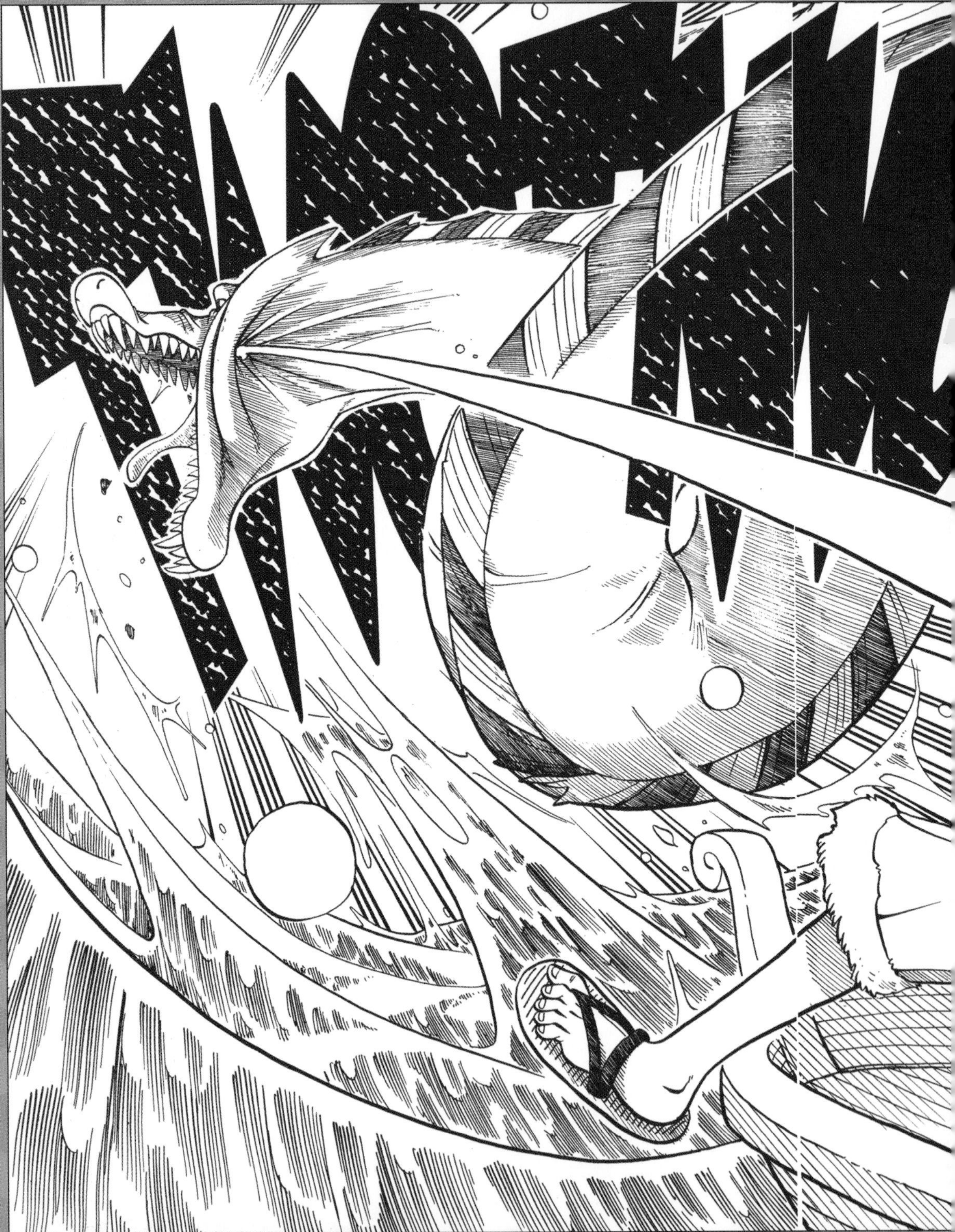

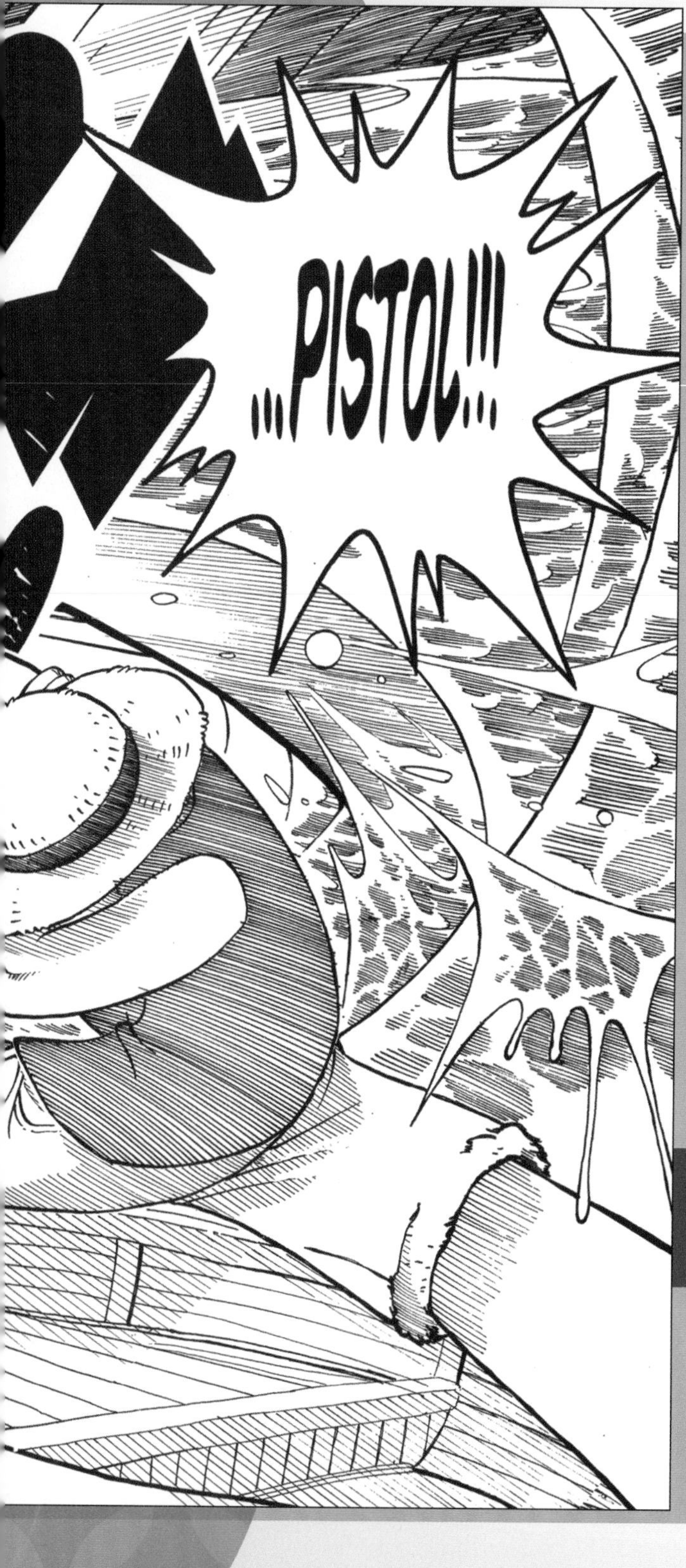
...PISTOL!!!

KŌKA-SEN (EFFECT LINES)

Kōka-sen are lines that indicate speed and power in a scene. There are various types of *kōka-sen.* The thickness, length, strength, and spacing between lines can vary to create different effects. *Kōka-sen* are used to enhance scenes by creating more excitement, movement, and momentum. They also help express a psychological state and guide the reader's eyes.

Example of *kōka-sen* in *One Piece*, courtesy of VIZ Media

THE FIVE CATEGORIES OF MANGA
マンガのカテゴリー

There are many reasons manga attracts fans from around the world. Manga may describe appealing worlds in which human fantasies have come true, such as the ability to travel across time or interact with aliens. Readers easily relate to the characters, both good and evil, with their interesting and detailed backstories. Most importantly, manga stories are diverse, often with profound story lines and masterful character development.

Character development—the protagonists' emotional, physical, and mental growth as a result of their actions and experiences—is a key component of Japanese manga. The emphasis on character development makes manga unique and complex but also relatable to readers.

Historically, Japanese stories have focused not only on the strength of the characters. The sadness and weaknesses characters experience are also crucial to the plot. Classical Japanese literature tends to lean toward sad stories in which the main character faces something tragic. These tragedies also occur in manga—some popular characters don't experience happy endings. One example is Leo, the main character in *Jungle Emperor* (*Jungle Taitei*, 1950), who grows from a cub into a mature lion. Leo lives through different generations of the lion family and eventually becomes emperor of the jungle, protecting the other animals from humans. Ironically, in the end, he gives up his flesh and skin to save a human friend, and only his fur remains. Osamu Tezuka gave him the body of a dying being, something not previously seen in manga characters.

Manga can be divided into five main categories based on target audience demographics. But regardless of category, individual readers will choose what attracts them.

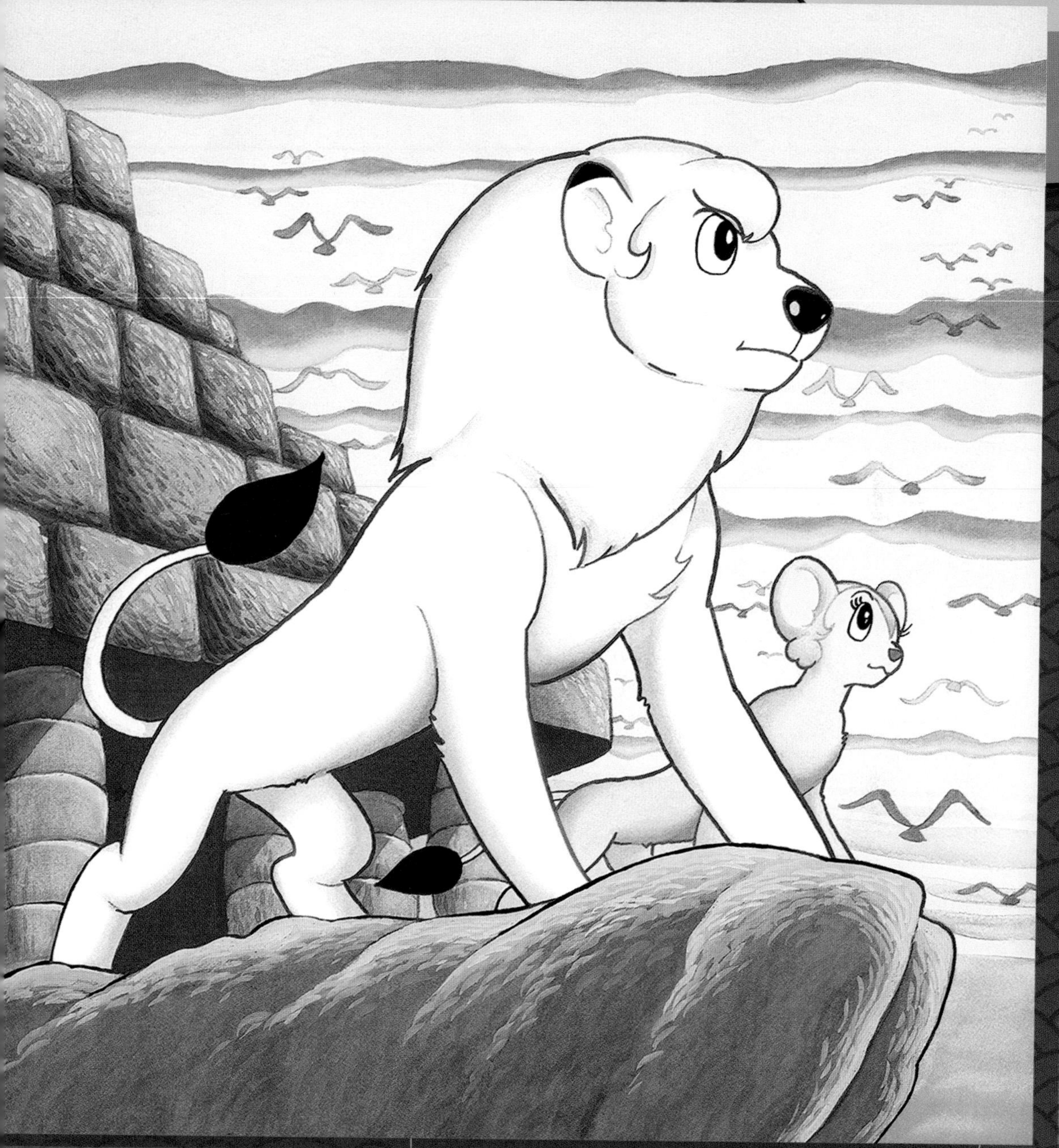

Art from *Jungle Emperor*. Courtesy of Tezuka Productions

1. *JIDŌ* (OR *KODOMO*) MANGA

These manga are intended for small children (*kodomo*) and elementary school students (*jidō*). Examples include *Anpanman*, in which Anpanman (*anpan* is a Japanese pastry with sweet red bean paste), comes to the aid of the hungry.

2. *SHŌNEN* MANGA

Shōnen (meaning boys) manga mainly targets boys but also attracts many adults and female readers. The plots, usually involving adventure or action stories, show how the main characters overcome their challenges. An example is the adventure story *One Piece*, in which the character Luffy seeks to become the Pirate King.

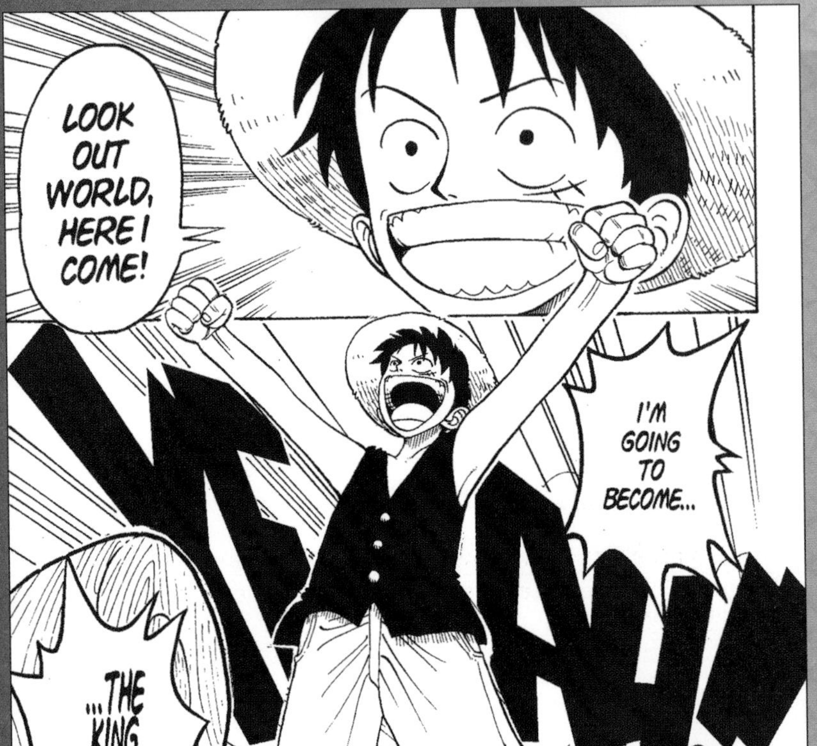
LOOK OUT WORLD, HERE I COME!
I'M GOING TO BECOME...
...THE KING OF THE PIRATES!!!!
LUFFY'S TINY BOAT FLOATS ON, HIS CREW YET TO BE FOUND...
LUFFY'S GREAT VOYAGE OF DESTINY HAS BEGUN!!!

A panel from *One Piece*, courtesy of VIZ Media

3. *SHŌJO* MANGA

Manga published in magazines appealing to girls are called *shōjo* (meaning girls) manga and are known for specific attributes, such as characters with big eyes and backgrounds filled with twinkling stars and flowers. In addition to stories full of romantic elements, *shōjo* manga may be fantasy or horror oriented. One of the most famous works in this category is *Sailor Moon*. The story concerns Usagi, who transforms into Sailor Moon and fights to protect Earth from enemies trying to conquer it. Its friendship and love themes made this series popular with fans of all ages.

4. *SEINEN* MANGA

This category is intended mainly for young male adults (*seinen*) and adult readers. Many *seinen* manga portray a harsh reality in which the characters suffer and must work hard to achieve their goals. The themes often concern the lives of university students and working adults. History, business, and social themes are also popular in this category.

5. *JOSEI* MANGA

This manga category is intended for adult women in their 20s or older (*josei*). Both the author and the main character are usually female, and the content explores romance, working life, and family issues.

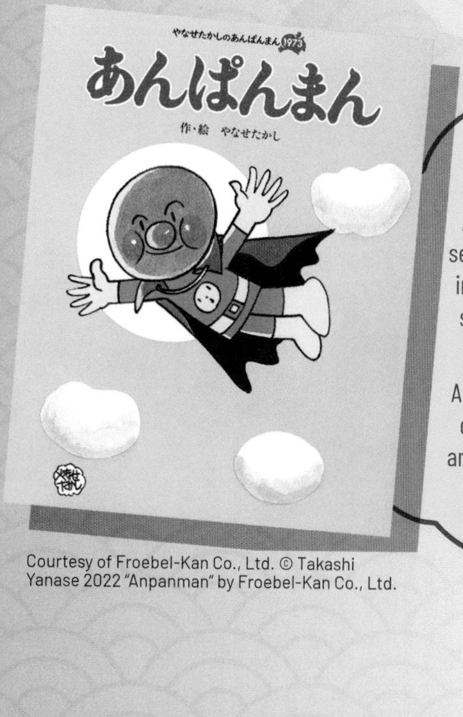
やなせたかしのあんぱんまん 1973
あんぱんまん
作・絵 やなせたかし

Courtesy of Froebel-Kan Co., Ltd. © Takashi Yanase 2022 "Anpanman" by Froebel-Kan Co., Ltd.

SO SUGOI!

Anpanman, created by Takashi Yanase, is one of the most popular hero series among children. Anpanman is a character from a picture book, and in 1988 was made into a TV anime series featuring loads of characters—so many that the 2009 Guinness World Records recognized it as having the "most characters in an animation series," 1,768 at the time!

Anpanman is an unusual hero. He feeds the hungry by tearing off chunks of his face for them to eat. The author went hungry during World War II and felt hunger was the most painful thing a human could endure. Yanase created Anpanman from such an experience.

THE ORIGINS OF MANGA
マンガの誕生

The origins of manga can be traced back to a set of four picture scrolls created in the 12th and 13th centuries called *Scrolls of Frolicking Animals and Humans* (*Chōjū-Jinbutsu-Giga*). In this series of images, the first of which appeared more than 800 years ago, animals imitate humans and humorously poke fun at the society of that time. The main characters, vividly depicted in ink, are rabbits, frogs, and monkeys. The animals' expressions

Panel from *Scrolls of Frolicking Animals and Humans*

Panel from *Scrolls of Frolicking Animals and Humans*

and gestures reveal their personalities so viewers can imagine who is cunning and who is naughty! At first, historians believed the artist behind the scrolls was a monk called Toba Sōjō. However, the lack of consistency in the drawing style convinced experts that the scrolls were the work of several artists.

The *Scrolls of Frolicking Animals and Humans* contain no text, only pictures. They are examples of *emakimono*, a narrative picture scroll; as the scroll progresses from right to left, the timeline and the story evolve. Viewers move from one scene to the next at their own pace, like readers who view manga today. The techniques of expression used in *emakimono* scenes carried over to modern manga. For example, lines are drawn from the mouths of the characters to indicate they are speaking, although no words are displayed.

SO SUGOI!

In 2016, Studio Ghibli (pronounced *gee-blee*), famous for the anime films *My Neighbor Totoro* and *Spirited Away*, animated the *Scrolls of Frolicking Animals and Humans* for a TV commercial. The cute images depict a rabbit and a frog, both famous characters, having a wonderful encounter on a rainy day.

During Japan's Edo period (1603–1867), with the development of printing technology, *Toba-e* became popular in Osaka, a city in western Japan. *Toba-e* are comical paintings that depict everyday life (the word *Toba* comes from Toba Sōjō, one of the artists of the centuries-old scrolls). The figures in *Toba-e* have long arms and legs, eyes with black circles or single letters, large mouths, and exaggerated movements. They are dynamic and resemble some modern manga characters, don't you think?

Toba-e soon spread to Edo (present-day Tokyo). Since the drawings mostly depicted the lives of ordinary people, they were readily appreciated by the general public. In 1814, *Hokusai Manga* was published by Hokusai, a well-known *ukiyo-e* artist (*ukiyo-e* means "pictures of the floating world" and refers to a style of Japanese woodblock printing). *Hokusai Manga* was an instructional book of 4,000 drawings of people, animals, plants, buildings, landscapes, and so much more. Hokusai apparently used the word *manga* to describe his random drawings of things.

Toba-e drawing

Example of *Hokusai Manga*

KUSAZŌSHI

There were also illustrated entertainment books called *kusazōshi*, which thrilled children in the Edo period. In the early days, most of these were illustrated picture books only for children, but over time witty and funny books were published for adults. *Kusazōshi* were classified according to the color of the cover and the contents.

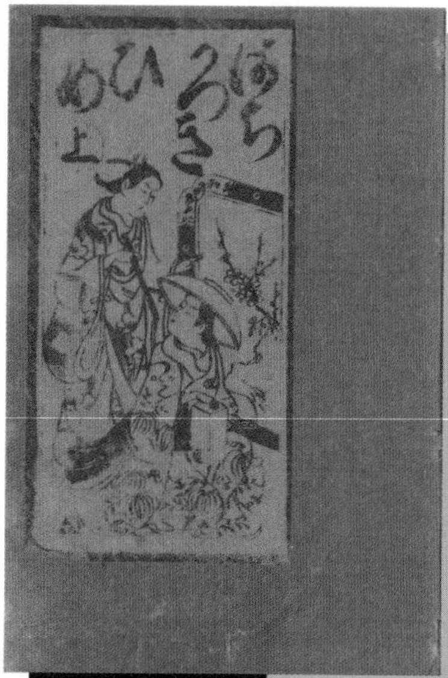

Akahon book

AKAHON (Red Book)

Akahon were illustrated books mainly for children with an educational element, such as folktales.

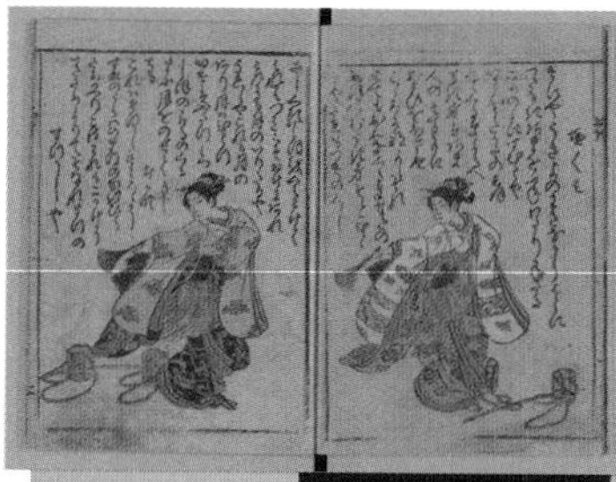

Kurohon book

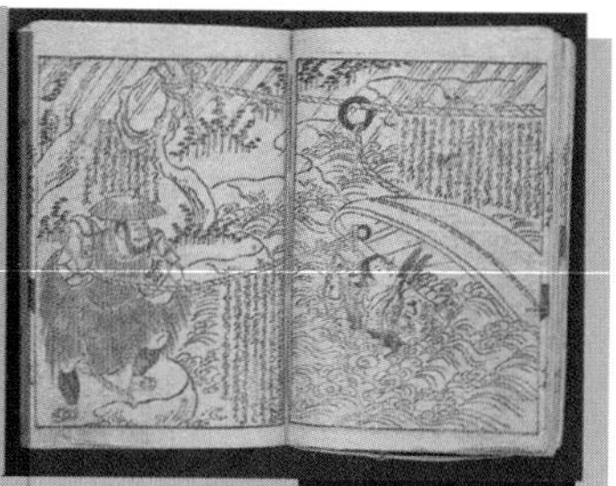

Aohon book

KUROHON (Black Book) AND *AOHON* (Blue Book)

These books targeted older readers and had diverse content, such as history, legendary heroes, and ghost stories.

KIBYŌSHI (Yellow Cover)

Kibyōshi had substantial entertainment value for adults, and their content was a mixture of humor, comedy, and satire. The illustrations included *fukidashi* (speech balloons), a technique of expression commonly found in modern manga.

Left: *Yōkai* from the Bakemono Zukushi handscroll. Right: *Amabie*.

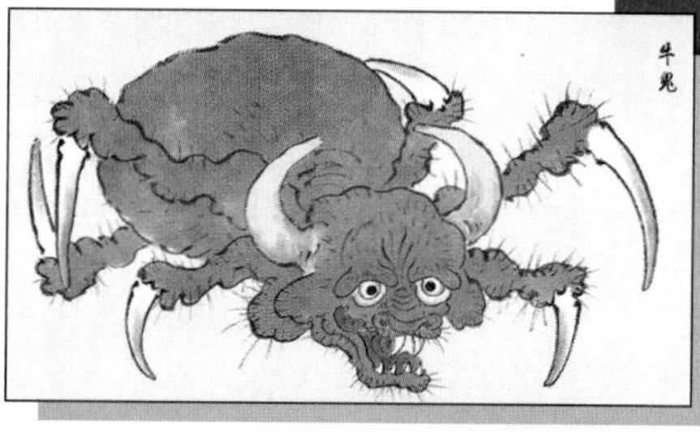
牛鬼

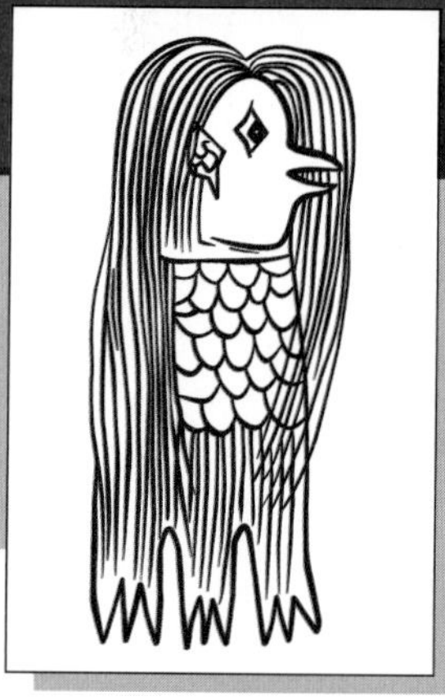

YŌKAI

Kusazōshi frequently depicted stories of ghosts and *yōkai* (supernatural beings and folktale creatures). Today, few people believe in the existence of *yōkai*, but many readers still enjoy them through manga and anime. Some *yōkai* are cute characters, such as those in *Yo-Kai Watch*, while others have terrifying appearances, like the ones in Shigeru Mizuki's *Kitaro*. Recently, due to the COVID-19 pandemic, *amabie*, a *yōkai* that protects against plagues, became very popular in Japan, especially on social networking sites.

EAST MEETS WEST: THE BEGINNINGS OF MODERN MANGA

現代マンガのはじまり

Many *Hokusai Manga* images are intriguing and resemble today's manga, but they lack an essential element: They do not tell a story. So, what opened the door to the manga we know today? Surprisingly, foreign cartoons!

During the Edo period, the Japanese government ended almost all trade with foreign countries and closed Japan to the outside world. This isolation began in the 17th century and lasted more than 200 years! In 1853, after US Navy Commodore Matthew Perry sailed into Tokyo Harbor, Japan finally reopened its borders to the outside world. As more foreigners visited, they introduced new customs that strongly impacted Japanese culture.

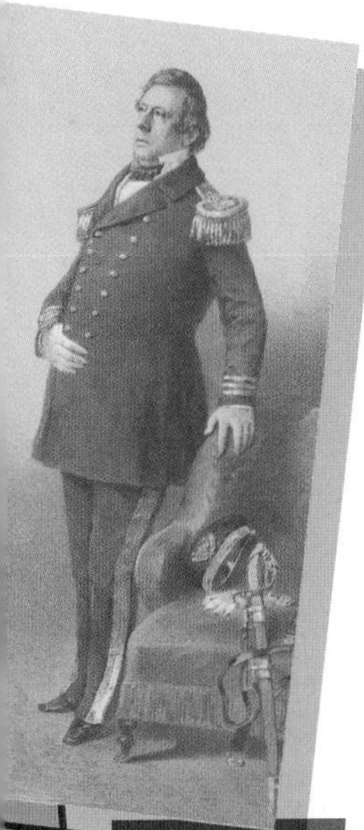

US Navy Commodore Matthew Perry

The origins of modern manga are evident in Japan's first humor magazine, *Japan Punch*, published in 1862 in a foreign settlement in Yokohama. The magazine, created by the Englishman Charles Wirgman, poked fun at Japanese customs and contemporary trends, mimicking the British satirical comic magazine *Punch*. Japanese people liked the magazine and started calling its caricatures *ponchi-e* ("Punch drawings").

Japanese manga culture expanded through the steady adoption of foreign elements. As the focus shifted from satire to humor, and pictures to stories, manga culture began to prosper. Many *manga-ka* emerged, and they created *yon-koma* (four-frame) *manga* in newspapers.

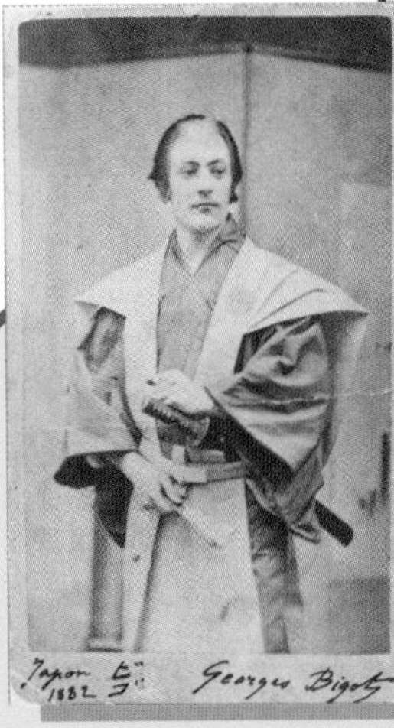
Japan 1882
Georges Bigot

SO SUGOI!

In 1887, the Frenchman Georges Bigot founded the satirical magazine *Tôbaé* (a name derived from *Toba-e*, mentioned in the previous chapter). He came to Japan with a passion for Japanese art and published his magazine for French people living in Japan. He loved Japanese culture so much that you can find pictures of him dressed as a samurai!

THE LATE MR. CHARLES WIRGMAN, ARTIST, OF YOKOHAMA, JAPAN.

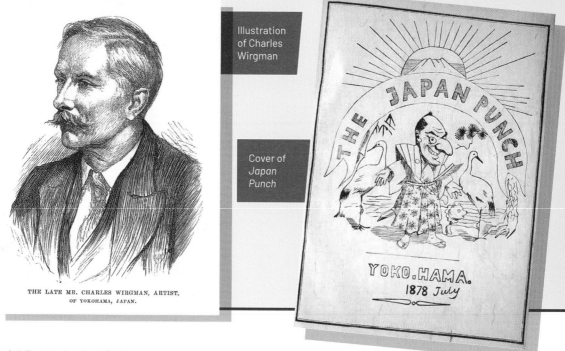

Illustration of Charles Wirgman

THE JAPAN PUNCH
YOKO.HAMA.
1878 July

Cover of *Japan Punch*

YON-KOMA MANGA

Yon-koma manga tell humorous stories. They have four frames arranged from top to bottom and often appear in Japanese newspapers. Nowadays, this type of manga is also popular in other media such as magazines and webcomics.

When the first daily newspapers in Japan launched in the late 19th century, there were few illustrations to explain the news content. Later, to attract more readers, they added cartoons. These cartoons made the newspapers more accessible and popular. Most newspaper readers were adult men at the time, but the entertaining cartoons encouraged women and children to check out the newspapers, too.

In 1923, the *Asahi Shimbun* newspaper began serializing Japan's first *yon-koma manga*, *The Adventures of Shō-chan* (*Shō-chan no Bōken*), illustrated by Katsuichi Kabashima. This *yon-koma* followed a brave boy named Shō-chan and his squirrel companion through a fairyland. His adventures were immensely popular with children and adults. *The Adventures of Shō-chan* was first published while the trauma of the Great Kantō Earthquake was still fresh in people's minds. This manga was a soothing and comforting presence for readers in the dark days following that disaster.

The newspapers produced a number of hits, including *Fuku-chan*, created by Ryūichi Yokoyama in 1936 and featuring a mischievous boy in a kimono, *geta* (wooden clogs), and a large school cap; and *Sazae-san*, created by Machiko Hasegawa in 1946 about the daily life of Sazae, a housewife living in Tokyo with her family. *Yon-koma manga* continued to appear in newspapers and provide readers with moments of distraction from everyday life.

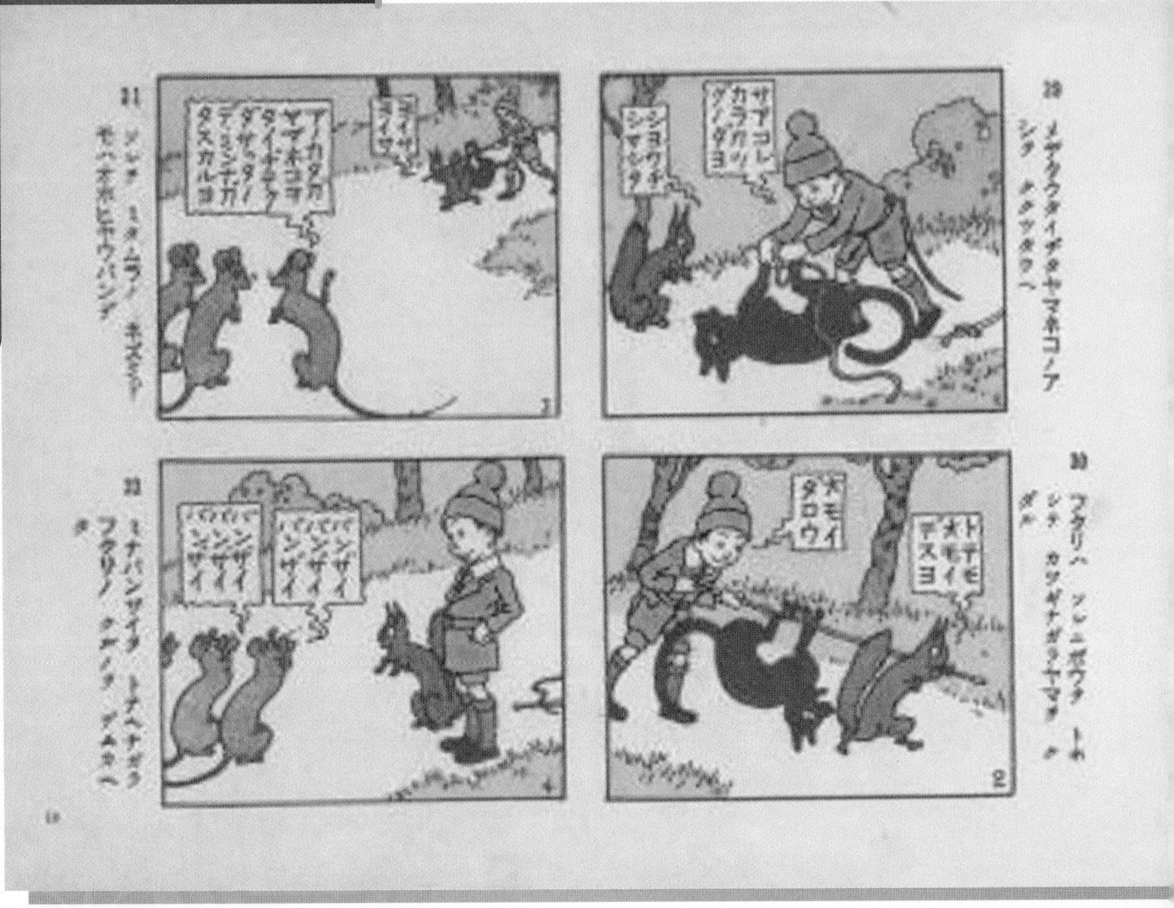

Children surrounding a *kamishibai*

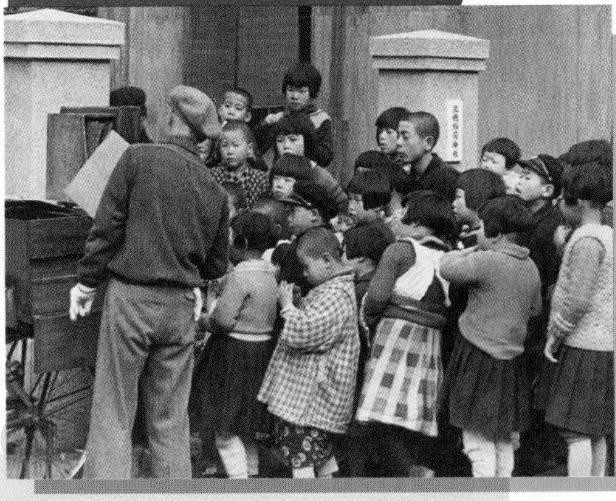

KAMISHIBAI

Around 1930, the art form *kamishibai* (paper drama) began to flourish in Japan. In *kamishibai*, a performer tells a story while displaying pictures one at a time. A *kamishibai-ya* (storyteller) with *kamishibai* panels on the back of his bicycle would go to an alley or park and call the children over. In return for purchasing candy, rice crackers, and other sweets, the children could view the *kamishibai* show. The storytelling included historical dramas, detective/adventure stories, science fiction, and many other genres. It was a source of entertainment for children in the days before TV until the 1950s.

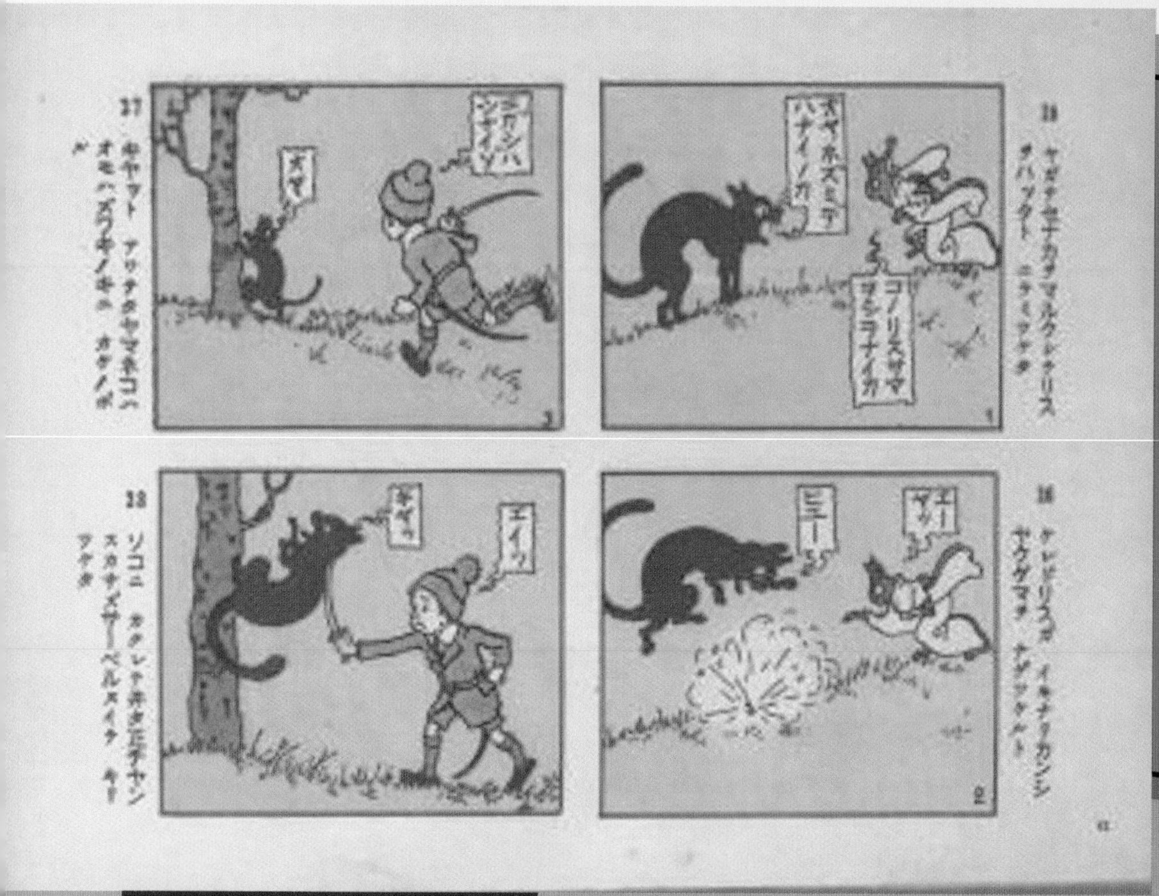

Panels from *The Adventures of Shō-chan*

Kamishibai surged in popularity with the story of *Golden Bat* (*Ōgon Batto*), which first appeared in 1931. This science fiction tale set in the future was original: The hero was a skull-masked Bat who fought an evil organization. This costumed hero was a pioneer of today's transformable heroes and was introduced earlier than Superman and Batman, who first made their appearances in the late 1930s. Golden Bat's stories became so popular that they were made into manga, anime, and live-action films.

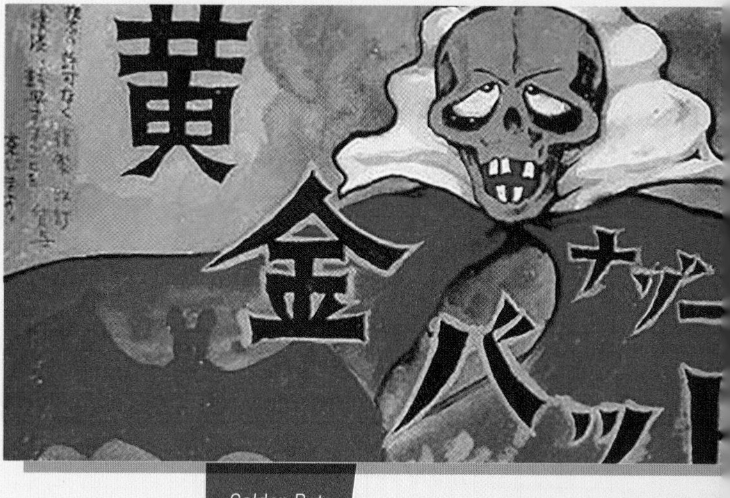
黄金バット

Golden Bat

SO SUGOI!

Kobo-chan, created by Masashi Ueda and first published in 1982, surpassed 14,000 comic strips in 2022, making it the most serialized manga ever published in a Japanese newspaper. *Kobo-chan* is a family manga with many heartwarming episodes. On March 12, 2011, the day after the Great East Japan Earthquake and Tsunami, the manga depicted peaceful everyday life to help ease people's minds amid the pervasive sadness.

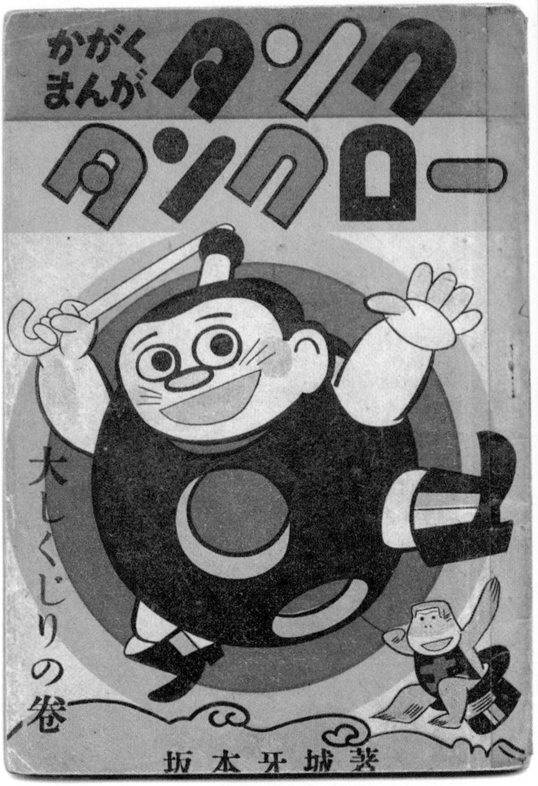
かがく
まんが
タンク
タンクロー
大しくじりの巻
坂本牙城著

Above: Cover to a volume of *Tank Tankurō*. Courtesy of the estate of Gajo Sakamoto and Presspop Inc.

PRE–WORLD WAR II MANGA

Children's manga was an influential genre just before the war, and many war-inspired manga were produced, most notably *Norakuro*, created by Suihō Tagawa in 1931. Norakuro, a stray dog with no family, enlists in a dog army. Children root for him as he rises to the rank of captain cheerfully and energetically, undeterred by his circumstances. Norakuro's face was printed on all kinds of stationery and on a variety of collectibles. Techniques used in *Norakuro* greatly influenced later manga, including symbols such as the dust cloud that swells up after walking and the star that indicates a crash.

Tank Tankurō, created by Gajo Sakamoto in 1934, featured one of the first superheroes to appear in manga: a robot of the same name who used special tools and gimmicks that popped out of his body to help him defeat the bad guys. People regard *Tankurō* as the first science fiction manga and one that influenced *Astro Boy*.

In the early 1940s, as World War II intensified, manga disappeared from major newspapers, and manga magazines ceased publication.

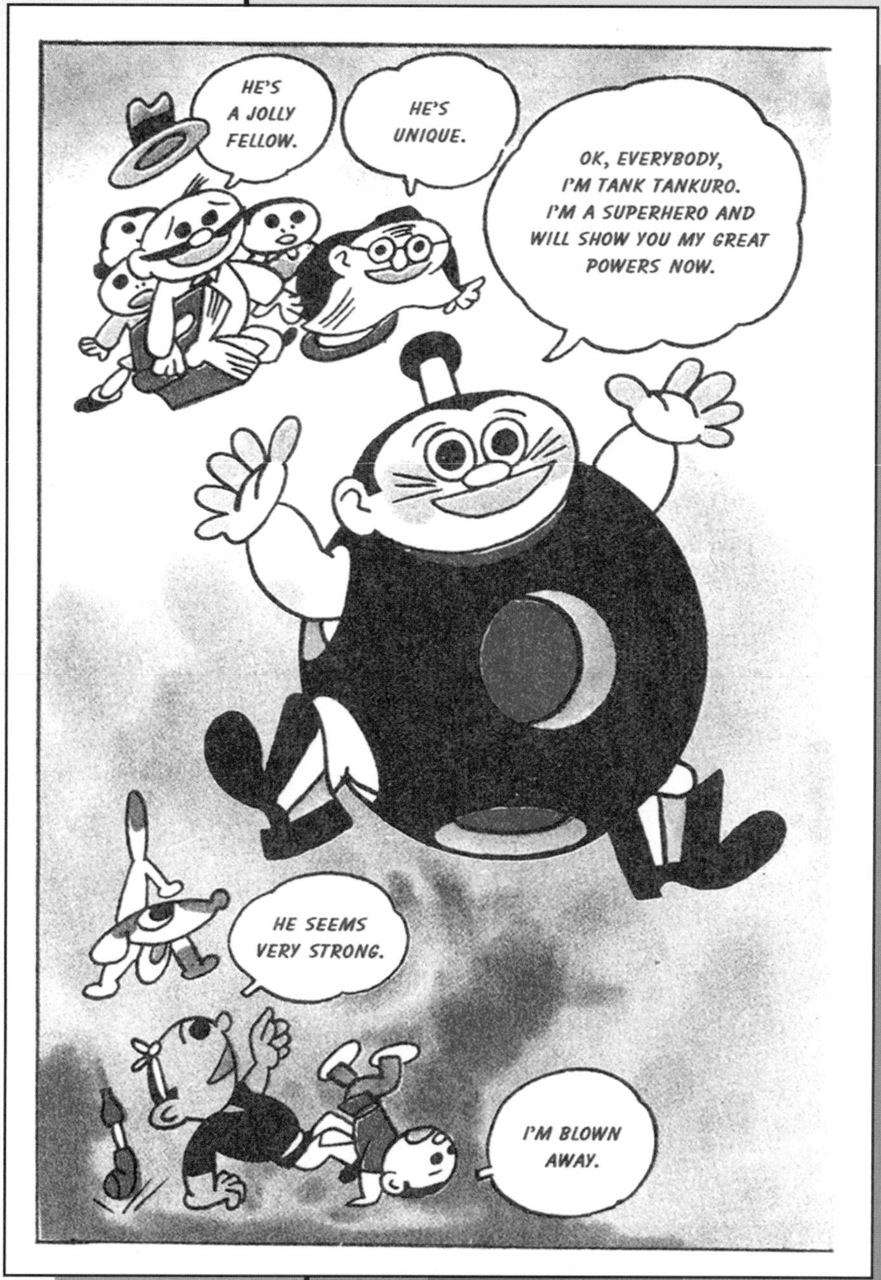
OK, EVERYBODY, I'M TANK TANKURO. I'M A SUPERHERO AND WILL SHOW YOU MY GREAT POWERS NOW.
HE'S UNIQUE.
HE'S A JOLLY FELLOW.
HE SEEMS VERY STRONG.
I'M BLOWN AWAY.

Above: A page from *Tank Tankurō*. Courtesy of the estate of Gajo Sakamoto and Presspop Inc.

AFTER THE WAR: MANGA IN THE 1950S
戦後のマンガ

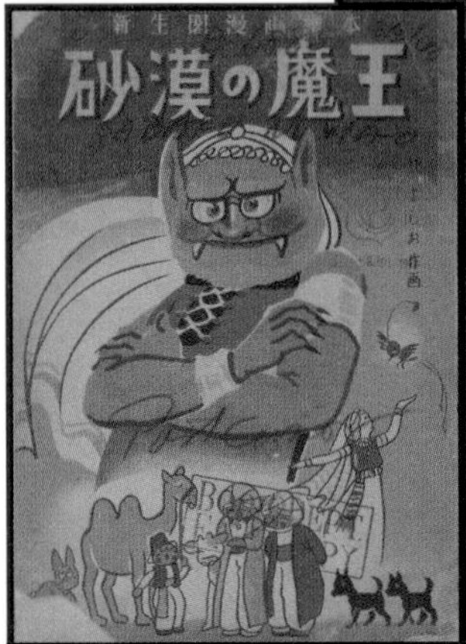
砂漠の魔王

An *akahon* manga, courtesy of Gordon W. Prange Collection, University of Maryland Libraries

AKAHON AND KASHIHON-YA

With World War II's end in 1945, the history of manga was once again on the move; manga magazines were being printed and *yon-koma manga* reappeared in newspapers. Undoubtedly, the *manga-ka* of the time wanted to help Japan recover from its wartime devastation.

Around this time, *akahon* were produced at a reduced cost and sold at festival fairs and candy stores. *Akahon manga* had reddish covers, which made them stand out on the shelf. The name *akahon* originated with popular children's books printed in the Edo period, and the same name was used to describe these inexpensive postwar manga. Over time, as the price of *akahon* rose, kids could no longer afford them, and they disappeared from shelves.

To replace *akahon*, *kashihon-ya* (book rental shops) started up and prospered. Books could be borrowed from *kashihon-ya* for 10 to 20 yen, the equivalent of 7 to 14 cents. Many young people seeking to become *manga-ka* brought their manuscripts to publishers who specialized in rental books because they wanted to draw more freely than the major publishers allowed. Many *manga-ka* who made their debut in this rental book industry later became famous.

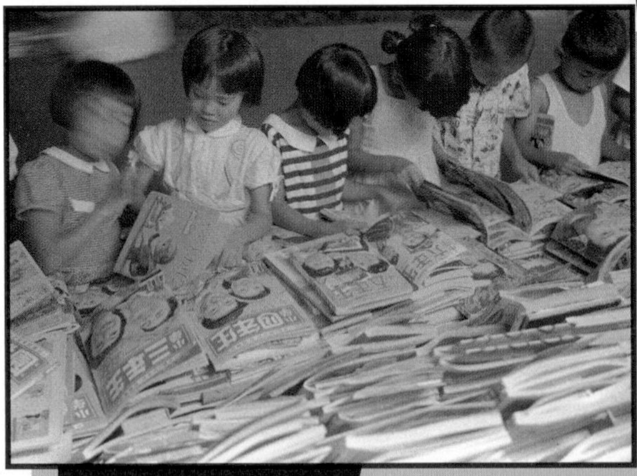

Children at a *kashihon-ya*

The manga produced at that time still influences *manga-ka* today. Many well-known *manga-ka* entered the field because they admired these earlier works. In this way, Japanese manga culture has been passed from one generation to the next. The lively manga culture of the 1950s led to the industry's explosive growth, and the translation of manga into many foreign languages spurred a worldwide craze.

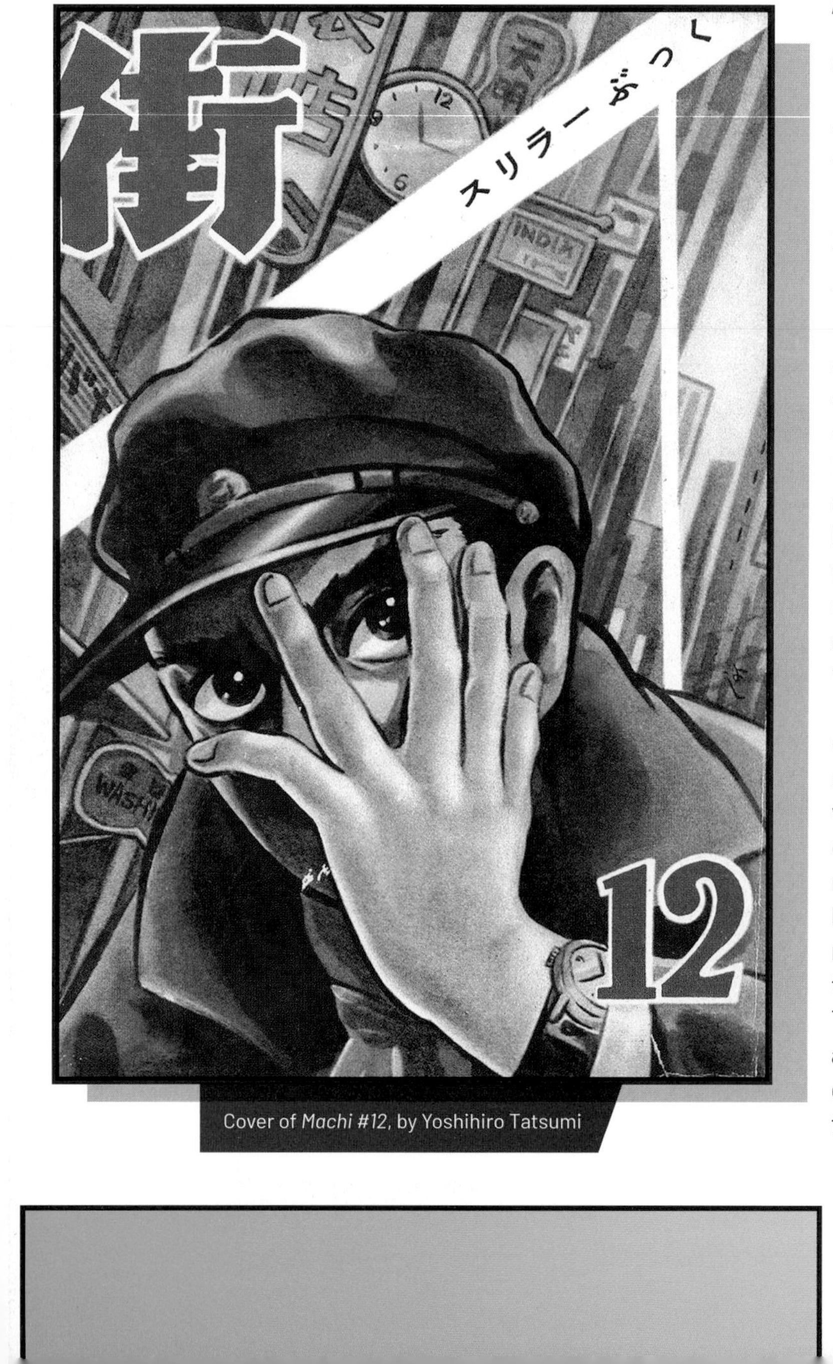
街
スリラーぶっく
12

Cover of *Machi #12*, by Yoshihiro Tatsumi

THE BIRTH OF *GEKIGA*

A new style of manga, known as *gekiga* (dramatic pictures), became popular during the *kashihon-ya* era. In 1957, Yoshihiro Tatsumi first used the term *gekiga* in his work *Ghost Taxi* (*Yūrei Taxi*). The story was action-packed, and the style of pictures was different from that found in children's manga. The story was more serious, less humorous, and featured psychological profiles and realistic drawings. This attracted mature readers and triggered a *gekiga* boom.

Gekiga was a major development in the history of manga. Previously, readers were considered to be too old for children's manga after middle school, but with the birth of *gekiga*, narrative manga expanded to include teenagers and young adults. Today, men and women of all ages enjoy a variety of manga genres, and the starting point for this expansion was *gekiga*.

MANGA BANNING

Barefoot Gen (*Hadashi no Gen*) is a manga about a second grader, Gen, who loses his family and home during the atomic bombing of Hiroshima in 1945. He experiences many hardships, helps the weak, and grows up with the support of friends in postwar Japan. The manga began serializing in 1973, and the author, Keiji Nakazawa, depicted his personal experiences of the atomic bombing. The work vividly describes the cruelty and tragedy of war and, at the same time, the resilience of human beings. To keep the story from becoming too serious, comedic episodes were introduced at critical points. Art Spiegelman, the author of *Maus*, the story of Jewish survivors of the Holocaust, was heavily influenced by Nakazawa and wrote in an introduction to the first English volume of *Barefoot Gen*, "[H]is work is humanistic and humane, demonstrating and stressing the necessity for empathy among humans if we're to survive into another century."

Barefoot Gen used to be available in classrooms and school libraries throughout Japan, where students could read it freely at any time. But in 2012, the Matsue City Board of Education made a major decision. Because *Gen* contains brutal depictions that could traumatize children, and because some readers said the depictions were not accurate reflections of reality, the board required all elementary and junior high schools in Matsue City to restrict access to the manga. This became big news in Japan, and various opinions were exchanged. Most objected to Matsue City's response, saying that the tragedy of the atomic bombing and war is a fact, no matter how extreme the expression, and that it is meaningful to teach the facts. In the end, due to a flood of criticism and complaints, Matsue City withdrew its restrictions and left the decision up to individual schools.

Nakazawa learned through the great sorrow of war that people make mistakes, and he expressed this in a straightforward manner in his manga. Perhaps it was his intention to let children who read his manga understand that people are not perfect but learn from their mistakes and that they should never forget this aspect of human behavior.

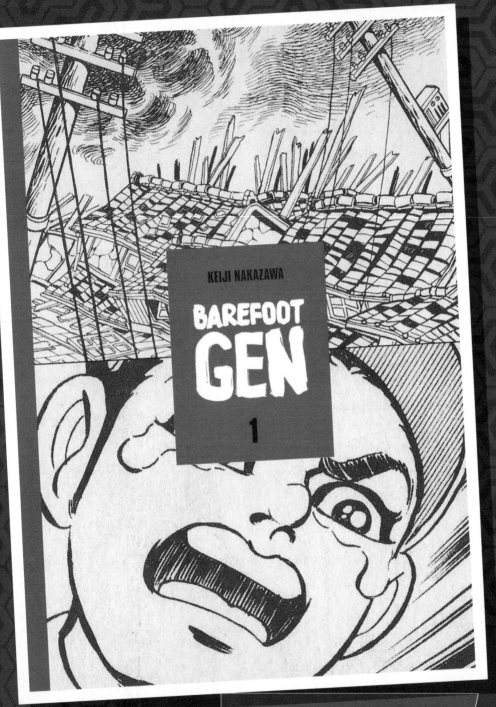

Cover (above) and panel from *Barefoot Gen*

© Keiji Nakazawa, reprinted by permission of the publisher,
Last Gasp of San Francisco

OSAMU TEZUKA AND TOKIWA-SŌ

手塚治虫とトキワ荘

Dreams, hopes, courage . . . the power of manga is inspirational and has evolved into a global culture. The "God of Manga," Osamu Tezuka, greatly expanded the possibilities of manga and was essential to establishing its status.

Osamu Tezuka (1928–1989) published a variety of manga books in Osaka after World War II. He was 18 years old when he wrote *New Treasure Island* (*Shin Takarajima*, 1947), which greatly impressed children at the time. It was published in a big volume 200-plus pages thick and became a bestseller, with 400,000 copies sold, prompting a nationwide *akahon* manga boom.

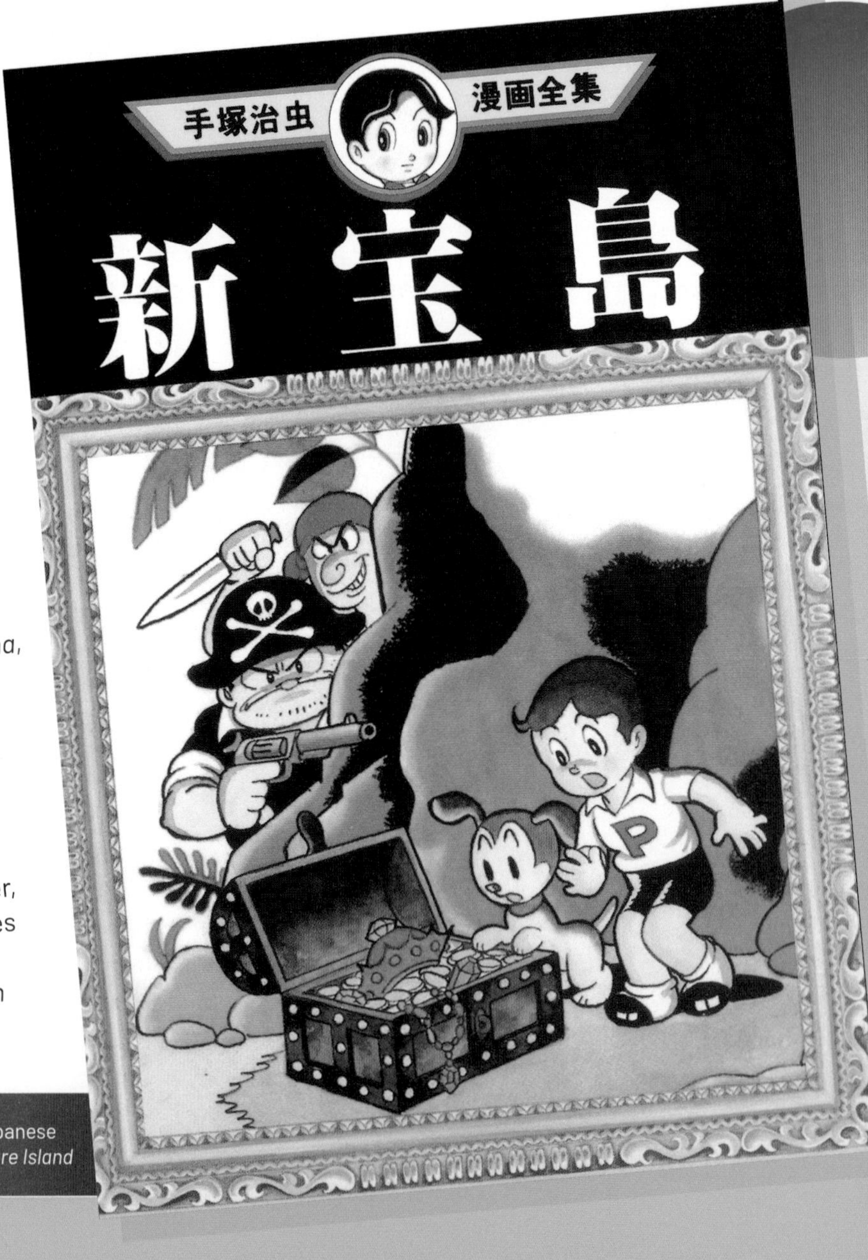
手塚治虫
漫画全集
新宝島
P

Cover of the 1984 Japanese edition of *New Treasure Island*

Tezuka not only established and revolutionized the manga world, but also modernized the foundations of manga by incorporating elements from Disney animations and movies into his work. To create his scenes, he used motion picture–like techniques and added a lot of dynamic action. His landmark works, such as the science fiction trilogy *Lost World*, *Metropolis*, and *Nextworld*, were full of themes related to science run amok and other threats to civilized society.

He produced a series of hits in the magazine world as well. Through easy-to-understand stories, Tezuka confronted society's problems, questioned discrimination, warned against the nuclear threat, and criticized political corruption. Beyond entertainment, his works were commentaries on social themes that examined how to live our lives with greater harmony and sincerity. He was a versatile artist but also a very prolific one, producing some 700 titles, including:

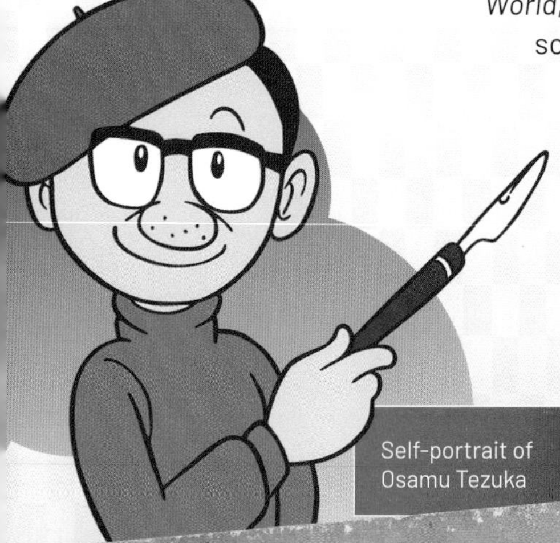

Self-portrait of Osamu Tezuka

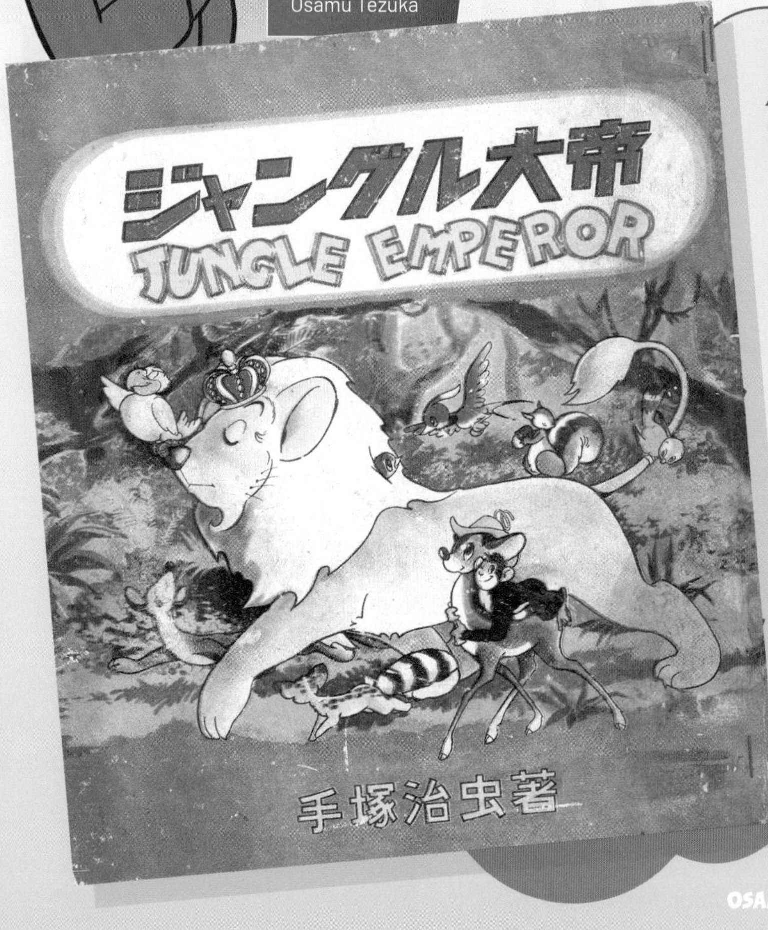
ジャングル大帝
JUNGLE EMPEROR
手塚治虫著

JUNGLE EMPEROR

(Janguru Taitei, 1950)

Leo, a white lion, is raised by humans. The manga depicts Leo, who understands human language, and his life after he succeeds his father as king of the jungle. It is an epic drama set in Africa about three generations of a legendary family of white lions.

All images courtesy of Tezuka Productions

ASTRO BOY

(*Tetsuwan Atomu*, 1952)

In a world where robots have emotions and rights like humans, the boy robot Astro uses his special abilities to defend people against evil beings, monster robots, and outer space invaders. He wonders what justice means in the face of human discrimination against robots but still keeps fighting to protect Earth and the people he loves.

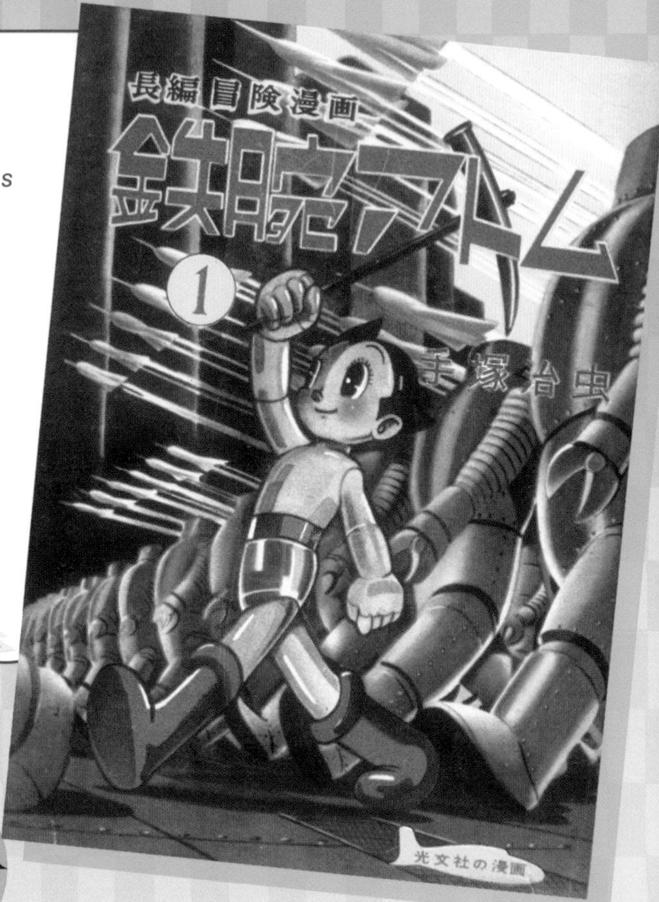
長編冒険漫画
鉄腕アトム
1
手塚治虫
光文社の漫画

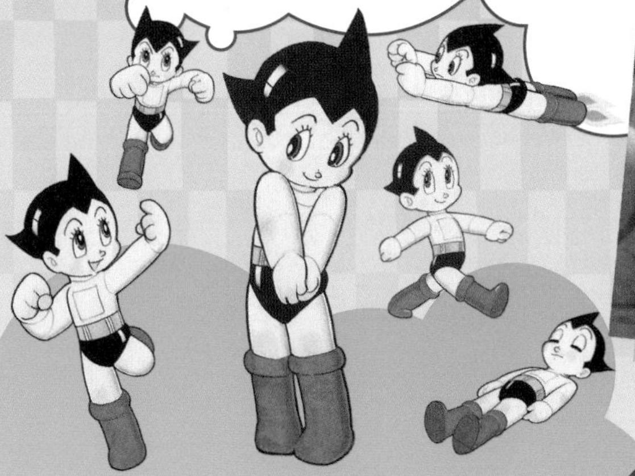

SO SUGOI!

The Takarazuka Revue was founded in 1913 and is one of the few all-woman musical theater companies in the world. They perform *Romeo and Juliet*, the American classics *Roman Holiday* and *Gone with the Wind*, and many works based on manga and anime, such as *The Rose of Versailles* and *Rurouni Kenshin*. In addition to female roles, this female theater company also takes on male roles. These spectacles employ large stage sets and glittering costumes that change from show to show.

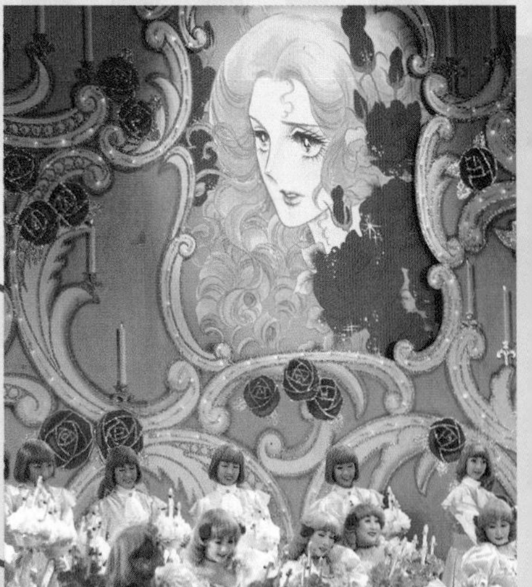

PRINCESS KNIGHT

(*Ribon no Kishi*, 1953)

Due to the mischief of an angel named Tink, Princess Sapphire is born with both the heart of a girl and a boy. However, because only a boy can occupy the throne, she is raised as a prince. On the day she succeeds her late father to the throne, it is revealed that Sapphire is a girl. Sapphire then dons a mask, dresses as a man, and, along with Tink, fights witches who torment people.

The story line was original at the time and pioneered the genre of girls' battle manga. Tezuka was an avid fan of the Takarazuka Revue (a theatrical troupe composed entirely of women)—his Sapphire character was inspired by how women play male roles in the theater.

講談社の漫画文庫
リボンの騎士
1
手塚治虫

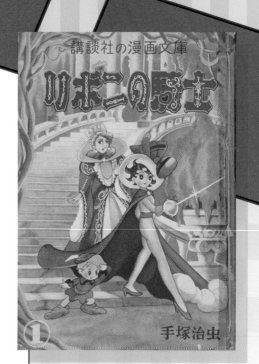

PHOENIX

(*Hi no Tori*, 1954)

A story based on the premise that if you drink the blood of a phoenix, you will become immortal. The story is set in both the past and the future and explores philosophical issues surrounding life and death, and reincarnation. Unfortunately, Tezuka passed away before completing this manga.

HINOTORI
火の鳥
手塚治虫
月刊 マンガ少年 別冊
1
黎明編

Astro Boy, *Princess Knight*, and *Phoenix* images courtesy of Tezuka Productions

Some of Tezuka's popular characters have round Mickey Mouse–like heads and big eyes, pointing to the strong influence of Disney cartoons in his work. However, in his manga, characters develop and grow up. The characters' feelings are on display, which makes it easier for readers to relate to them. At the time, it was very innovative to try and get manga readers to relate to and empathize with the protagonists.

An avid movie buff, Tezuka also developed a "star system." He treated his characters as if they were real movie actors. Just as one actor plays different roles in different movies, Tezuka had his characters star in various manga and in multiple roles. Until then, the protagonist of one manga never appeared or played a supporting role in another work. Tezuka seemed to enjoy playing the role of Hollywood director!

Tezuka was so busy that his manuscripts were often late, so his editor and colleagues had to step in and help complete them. That was the start of the assistant system in Japan, which is now commonplace in the industry. These days *manga-ka* cannot complete their work without the help of assistants. Tezuka's groundbreaking methods and innovations were passed on to his peers and to subsequent generations of *manga-ka*. They have become integral to modern manga production.

TOKIWA-SŌ

Tezuka's achievements in the manga industry are immeasurable. One great deed he performed was passing his knowledge and techniques on to future generations. Tokiwa-sō was an apartment building in Tokyo where Tezuka lived from 1953 to 1954. One by one, young *manga-ka* who admired Tezuka moved into the building, and it soon became a place where promising young *manga-ka* lived together, inspiring one another to perfect their talent, sensibility, and drawing techniques.

Left: Original Tokiwa-sō Building, courtesy of Mukaisasuke.

© Mukaisasuke

Right: Current Tokiwa-sō Manga Museum.

© Forward Stroke Inc.

Although Tokiwa-sō was demolished in 1982, an exact copy was rebuilt in 2020. It stands only a few minutes away from where the original stood and is now a major manga museum. Influenced by Tezuka, Tokiwa-sō members became Japan's leading *manga-ka*. Some of the residents were:

FUJIKO • F • FUJIO

(1933–1996)

In 1951 Hiroshi Fujimoto teamed up with Motoo Abiko, and they branded themselves "Fujiko Fujio" in 1954. The year after the duo broke up in 1987, Fujimoto changed his name to Fujiko • F • Fujio and continued writing mainly for Doraemon*, one of Japan's most amusing children's manga.* Doraemon *is a cat-shaped robot from the 22nd century who employs various futuristic tools to help Nobita, a boy who frequently messes up. The manga and its anime are very popular across Asia. Besides* Doraemon*, Fujimoto created many other comics dealing with science, aliens, and dinosaurs.*

TENTŌMUSI COMICS
てんとう虫コミックス
ドラえもん
第1巻
藤子・F・不二雄

ぼくだけど。
気にさわったかしら。
ワッ
だ、だれだっ!?
どこからきたんだ。
なにしに……。
ど、ど、どうしてこんなところから……。
いっぺんに聞かれてもこまるな。
そんなこと、どうでもいいじゃない。
ぼくはきみをおそろしい運命からすくいにきた。

Cover to the first volume of *Doraemon*, as well as a panel from the interiors

FUJIKO FUJIO Ⓐ (1934–2022)

Motoo Abiko excelled in a wide range of genres, including black humor, occult, fantasy, and sports. He tended to depict the dark side of human nature. After the separation of the duo Fujiko Fujio, Abiko's activities centered on youth manga under the pen name Fujiko Fujio Ⓐ. One of his best-known works is the black humor masterpiece The Laughing Salesman (Warau Salesman)*. It is the story of a mysterious salesman, Fukuzō Moguro, and the lives of those who broke promises to him.*

SHŌTARŌ ISHINOMORI

(1938–1998)

In his second year of high school, Shōtarō Ishinomori submitted a manga to a magazine publisher, and it caught the eye of Osamu Tezuka, who hired him as an assistant for Astro Boy*. In the 1960s, his works* Cyborg 009 *and* Kamen Rider *became enormously popular. The* Kamen Rider *series was broadcast as live-action dramas abounding with special effects. This popular series continues even today.*

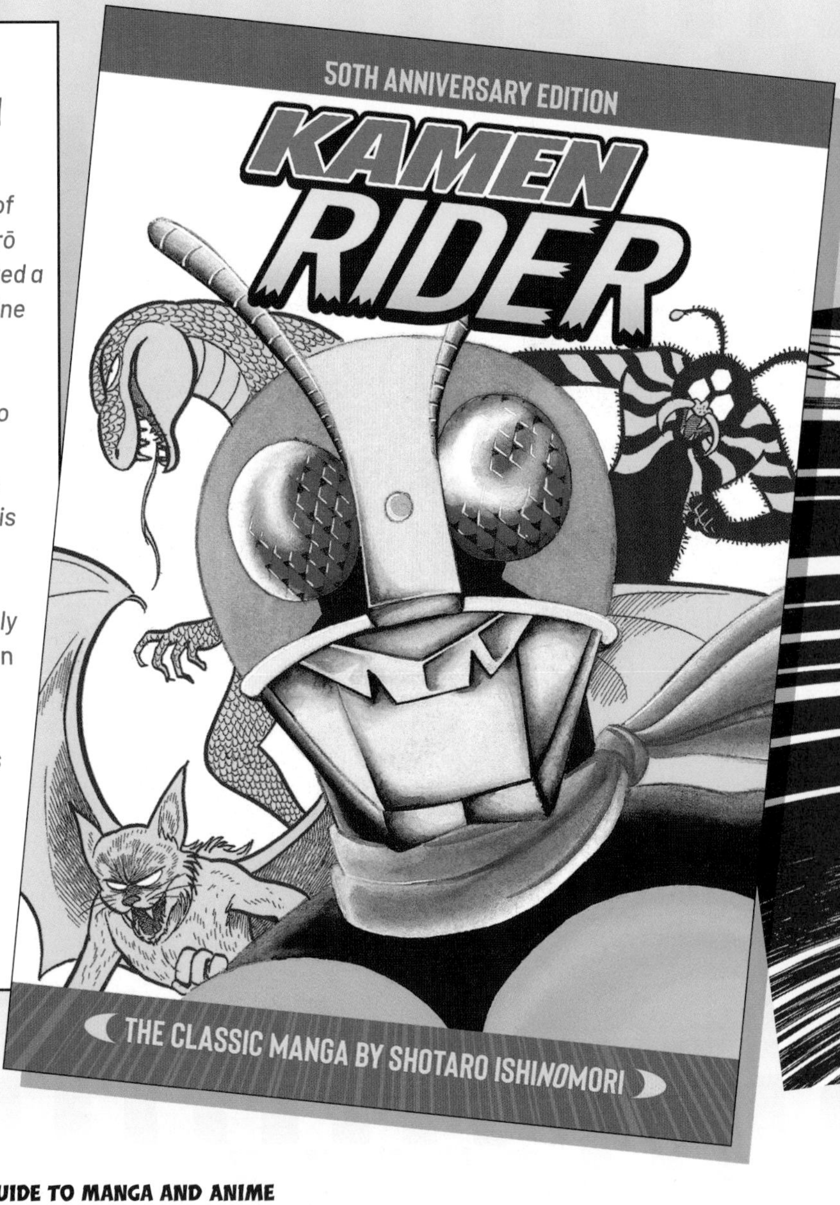
50TH ANNIVERSARY EDITION
KAMEN RIDER
THE CLASSIC MANGA BY SHOTARO ISHINOMORI

FUJIO AKATSUKA (1935–2008)

Fujio Akatsuka made his debut in 1956 with the shōjo manga Beyond the Storm *(Arashi o Koete), but his success with* Osomatsu-kun *and* The Secrets of Akko-chan *(Himitsu no Akko-chan) helped him become one of the most popular manga-ka. In 1967, his work* Tensai Bakabon *was also a big hit, and his recognition as a gag manga-ka spread rapidly. A genius at catchphrases, he was well-known for coming up with memorable buzzwords.*

Although not a resident of Tokiwa-sō, Mitsuteru Yokoyama (1934–2004) is another representative manga artist of this period. Inspired by Tezuka's *Metropolis*, Yokoyama pursued a career as a *manga-ka*. His representative works include the robot manga *Tetsujin 28 (Tetsujin 28-gō)*, which launched the giant robot anime genre, and *Sally the Witch (Mahōtsukai Sarī)*, which helped start the magical girl manga genre.

SO SUGOI!

In 2007, Guinness World Records recognized Ishinomori's complete works as the largest number of comics published by a single author worldwide: 770 titles in 500 volumes. That's over 128,000 pages!

Kamen Rider cover (left) and interior (above) courtesy of Seven Seas Entertainment

SHŌNEN MANGA THROUGH THE 1970S

1970年代までの少年マンガ

From the 1950s to the 1960s, manga magazines debuted one after another. On March 17, 1959, *Weekly Shōnen Sunday* and *Weekly Shōnen Magazine* launched on the same day to become Japan's first weekly manga magazines.

WEEKLY SHŌNEN SUNDAY (1959–)

Shogakukan, the publisher of *Weekly Shōnen Sunday*, chose to include the word *Sunday* in the magazine's title from the concept that "whenever you read the magazine, you will feel as cheerful as if it were Sunday, and as bright as the sun." Shogakukan managed to lure members of Tokiwa-sō, and so the magazine was blessed with blockbusters like *Osomatsu-kun* (by Fujio Akatsuka) and *Perman* (by Fujiko • F • Fujio) from the start. Other hits followed, such as *Giant Robo*, boosting sales in the 1960s and 1970s.

GIANT ROBO
(*Jaianto Robo*, 1967)

This was a science-fiction robot manga series by Mitsuteru Yokoyama. The giant robot GR1, operating under the command of a young man, Daisaku, fights off aliens plotting to invade Earth.

PERMAN

(Pāman, 1967)

This manga series created by Fujiko • F • Fujio follows an elementary school boy, Mitsuo, appointed as the apprentice superhero Perman—Superman without the Su. As Perman, he acquires tremendous strength and the ability to fly. He uses these powers to become a true superhero fighting for justice.

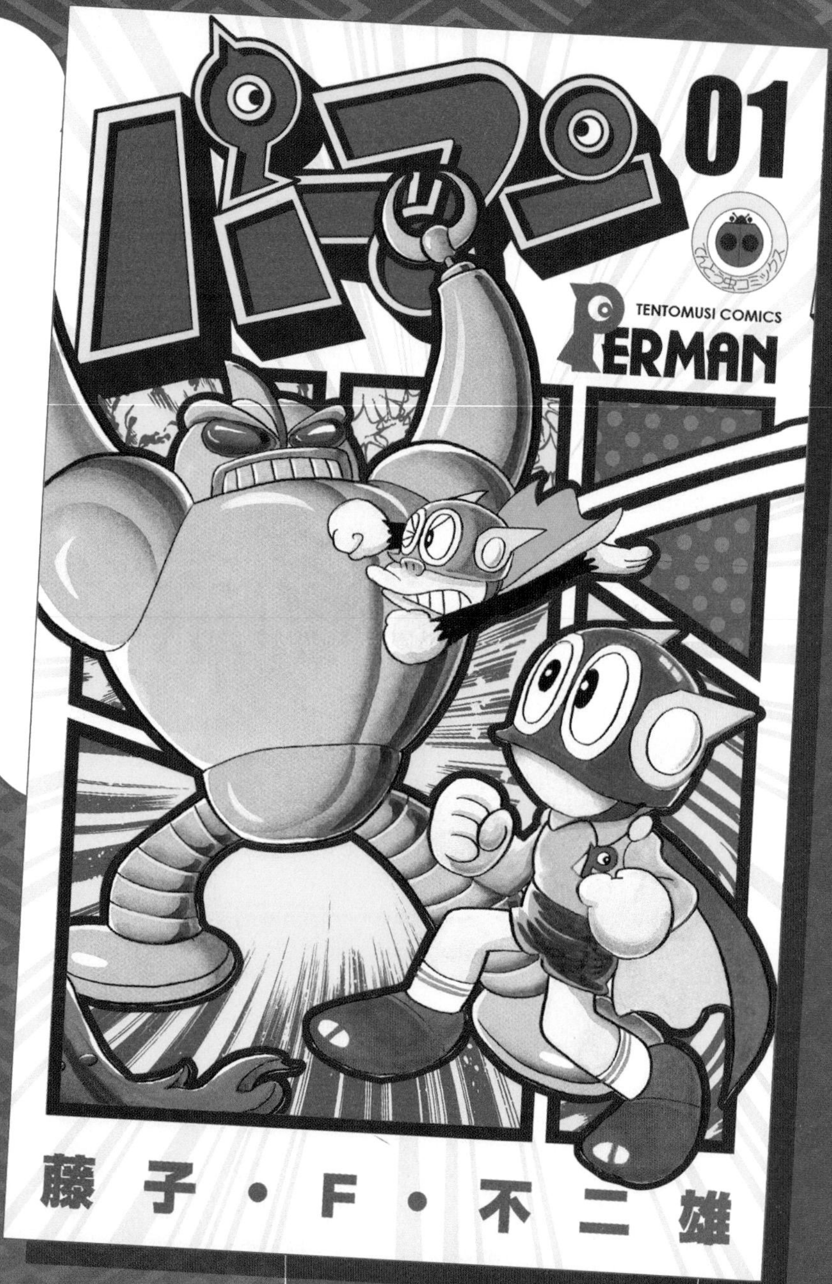
パーマン
01
てんとう虫コミックス
TENTOMUSI COMICS
PERMAN
藤子・F・不二雄

Cover of the first volume of *Perman*, courtesy of Fujiko-Pro and Shogakukan

WEEKLY SHŌNEN MAGAZINE (1959–)

Appearing with the catchphrase "Magazine of Dreams and Hopes," *Weekly Shōnen Magazine*, published by Kodansha, mainly produced serialized novels, and only a few manga works, in its debut. After its launch, the magazine lost sales to *Weekly Shōnen Sunday*; however, *Weekly Shōnen Magazine*'s sales skyrocketed with the massive success of the manga *Star of the Giants* and *Tomorrow's Joe*.

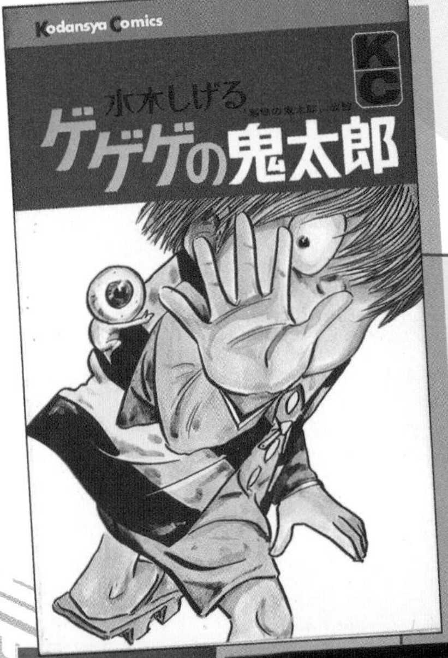
Kodansya Comics
KC
水木しげる
ゲゲゲの鬼太郎

STAR OF THE GIANTS

(*Kyojin no Hoshi*, 1966)

The main character, Hyūma Hoshi, is a gifted baseball player trained by his father, Ittetsu, who used to play third base for the Giants. It depicts the bond of father and son as Ittetsu helps Hyūma fend off fierce rivals to become the Giants' ace player.

KITARO

(*Gegege no Kitarō*, 1967)

This is the masterpiece of Shigeru Mizuki (1922–2015), the star of the yōkai manga genre. Centered around the main character Kitarō, the manga depicts the mayhem caused by a wide variety of yōkai. Most of the yōkai appearing in the series are based on folklore tales from different regions of Japan.

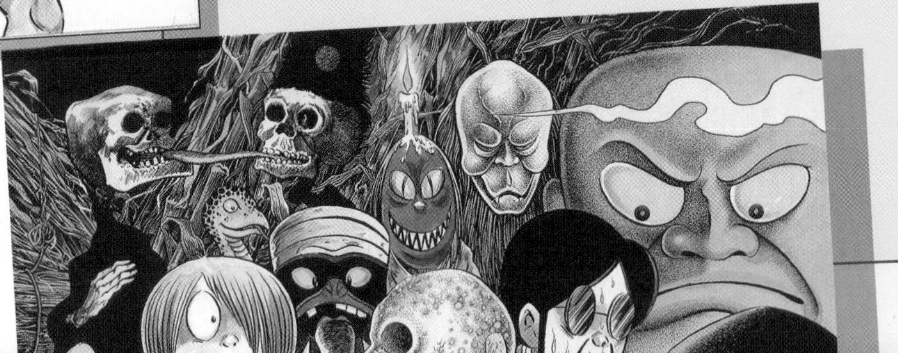

Cover of the first volume of *Kitaro*, as well as artwork, courtesy of Mizuki Productions

TOMORROW'S JOE

(*Ashita no Joe*, 1968)

In this sports manga created by Ikki Kajiwara, who also authored Star of the Giants, *Joe shows up on a whim in Tokyo's working-class district and knocks out an alcoholic ex-boxer, Danpei Tange. Tange sees in Joe's moves a natural boxing talent and struggles to turn him into a top-notch boxer. The manga had a significant impact on the actual boxing world.*

新しい漫画新幹線
少年ジャンプ
ぜんぶ漫画・ぜんぶ読切
くじら大吾 梅本さちお
毎月2回発行!
Jump No. 1
創刊号
8月1日号 90yen

Left: Cover of the first volume of *Weekly Shōnen Jump*, courtesy of Shueisha Inc.

Below: Example of a *Weekly Shōnen Jump* survey, courtesy of Shueisha Inc.

After the launch of *Weekly Shōnen Sunday* and *Weekly Shōnen Magazine* in 1959, a few other *shōnen* manga magazines joined the market. Besides providing children with entertainment, the growing manga magazine market offered many new *manga-ka* opportunities to showcase their talent.

郵便はがき
119-0159
東京都千代田区一ツ橋2-5-10
集英社 週刊少年ジャンプ編集部
8645
今週おもしろかったものは
おもしろかった順に番号で……
1 2 3
希望のプレゼントは……
Wチャンスは 欲しい方に丸をつけよう!
A B
①とじこみ付録/ジャンプヒーロー絶唱!スペシャルLIVEシール!
④ONE PIECE
⑨SAKAMOTO DAYS
⑲PPPPPP
㉔HUNTER×HUNTER
住所〒
電話番号
氏名
年齢

WEEKLY SHŌNEN JUMP (1968–)

In 1968, *Weekly Shōnen Jump* was launched by Shueisha to compete with the two market leaders, *Weekly Shōnen Sunday* and *Weekly Shōnen Magazine*. The magazine's keywords were "Friendship, Effort, and Victory." Since popular *manga-ka* were already working for the other magazines, *Weekly Shōnen Jump* decided to recruit newcomers and have them compete for a spot in the magazine.

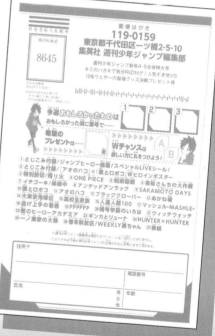

Using reader-based surveys, they identify the manga that readers most want to see and print them in the magazine. Their survey includes the question "Please write down the top three manga you enjoyed this week." This survey, which is still used today, ranks which works are the most popular each week. As a result, manga that do not rank well over a period of time are dropped. It sounds harsh, but that's how only the most popular works survive and how the magazine increases sales!

THE GUTSY FROG

(Dokonjō Gaeru, 1970)

In this comedy created by Yasumi Yoshizawa, a junior high school boy, Hiroshi, falls and crushes a frog under his chest. However, the frog, Pyonkichi, who gets flattened against Hiroshi's shirt, survives and lives with him, learning to speak human language.

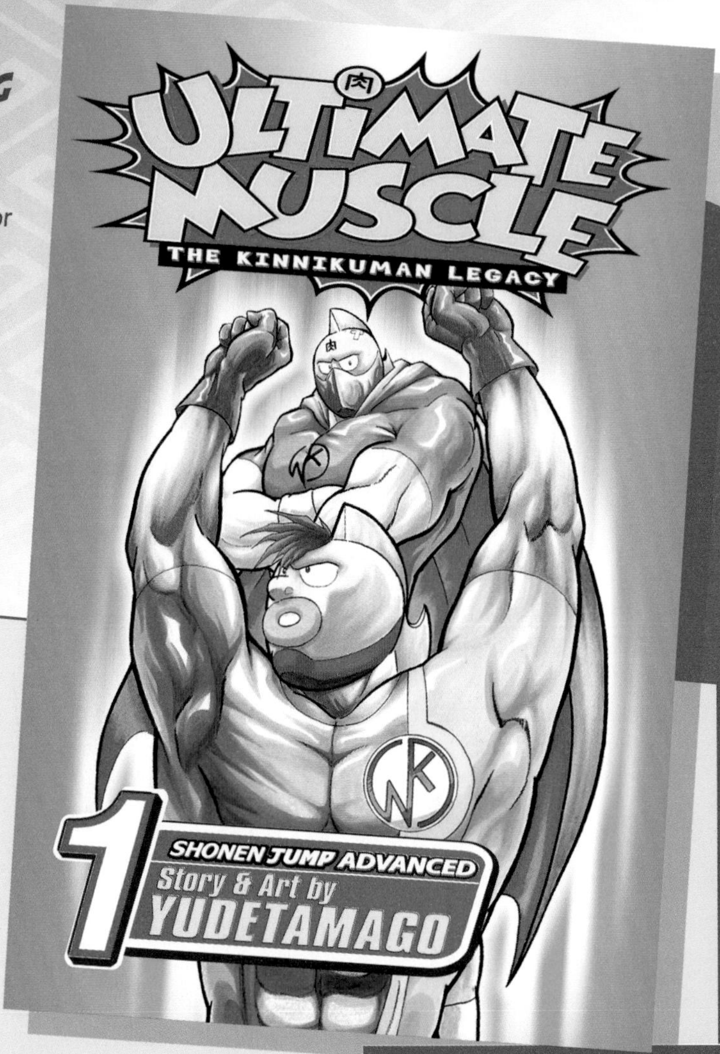

ULTIMATE MUSCLE
THE KINNIKUMAN LEGACY
1
SHONEN JUMP ADVANCED
Story & Art by
YUDETAMAGO

ULTIMATE MUSCLE

(Kinnikuman, 1979)

This is a very popular wrestling manga created by Yudetamago. Suguru Kinniku, a.k.a. Kinnikuman, is an outcast superhero who fights monsters and demons plotting to invade Earth. He matures through his friendships and awakens to his mission as a hero. Most of the character profiles are based on reader submissions.

Cover of the first volume of *Ultimate Muscle*, courtesy of VIZ Media

Since the 1970s, the consumption of manga by college students and young adults has been a fixture of youth culture. Looking to expand *shōnen* magazine circulation, publishers began adapting manga content to appeal to an older audience, hence the launch of *seinen* manga magazines targeting more mature readers.

SUPOKON

During the 1964 Tokyo Olympics and the years after, Japan saw a *supokon* boom. *Supokon* is an abbreviation for *supōtsu konjō* (fighting spirit in sports). Across Japan, people cheered on heroes who passionately pursued their dreams and developed as athletes. In addition to manga, many dramas and anime were broadcast with *supokon* themes drawn from the sports world, including baseball, volleyball, tennis, and judo.

Star of the Giants helped pioneer the *supokon* boom. Typical of *supokon* manga is the competition among rivals and the intense training required to win. In that era, the harsh training, too rigorous to be considered today, was depicted as a standard method for developing athletic skills. All the characters in *supokon* manga during that period acquired unique skills to help them defeat rival forces, like robot missiles or wizard magic.

It was not only through *shōnen* manga that *supokon* became nationally known. This surge in *supokon* also led to the publication of sports-oriented *shōjo* manga.

SO SUGOI!

In 2022, *Weekly Shōnen Sunday* and *Weekly Shōnen Jump* collaborated to feature characters from *Detective Conan* and *One Piece* on their covers. Both manga reached the 100th-published-volume milestone in 2021. They featured collaborative covers that created a single image when readers placed the two magazines side by side.

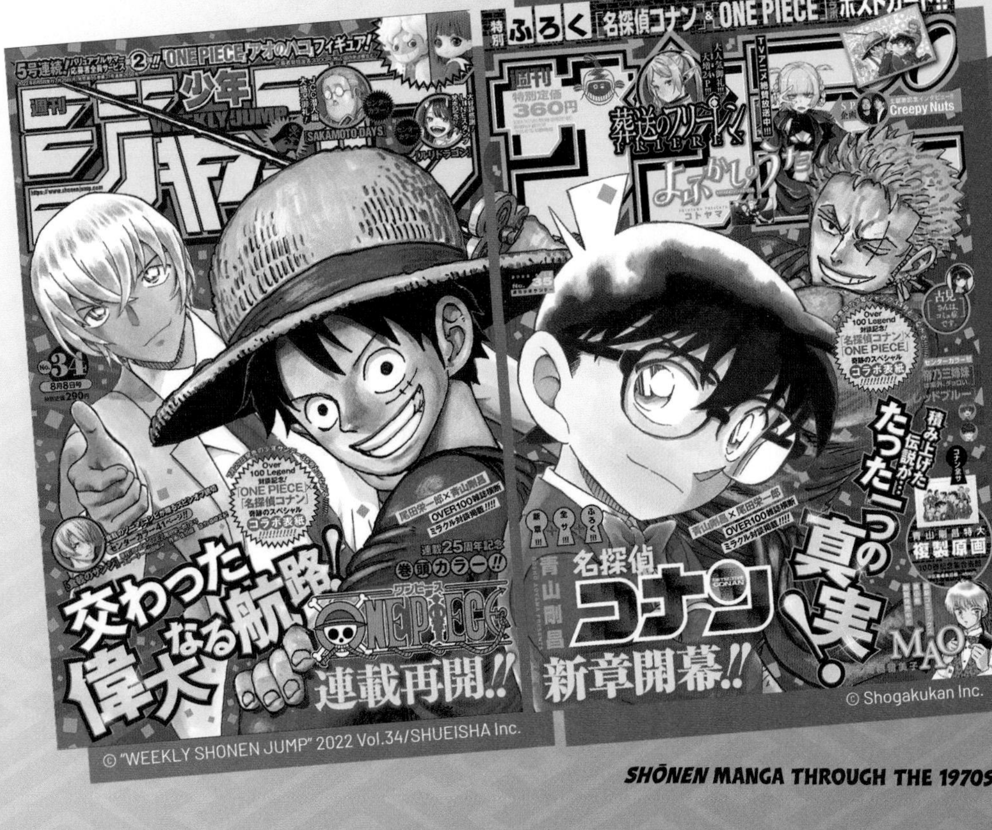

特別ふろく「名探偵コナン」&「ONE PIECE」ポストカード!!
5号連続!
少年
WEEKLY JUMP
SAKAMOTO DAYS
360円
Creepy Nuts
No.34
交わった偉大なる航路!
巻頭カラー!!
ONE PIECE
連載再開!!
名探偵コナン
新章開幕!!
積み上げた伝説が…
たった一つの真実!
MAO

SHŌJO MANGA THROUGH THE 1970S
1970年代までの少女マンガ

Female *manga-ka* work with great sensitivity to reflect contemporary trends; hence, their *shōjo* manga serve as a mirror of the times. As women's views on life, love, and their roles in society evolve, so do the heroines of *shōjo* manga. Over the years, *shōjo manga-ka* have expanded the range of this genre well beyond romance manga to include masterpieces of fantasy, science fiction, and fictional serious drama.

Similar to the action scenes and adventure stories in *shōnen* manga, *shōjo* manga have also developed unique qualities. Characters in *shōjo* are drawn delicately, many with beautifully illustrated silky hair or sparkling eyes. This elegance is also transmitted in a narrative technique

集英社の明かるく楽しい

少女ブック

二大ふろく
①特製 ひめ手箱
②机上立 フランス人形

創刊号

昭和26年8月創刊

Cover of the first issue of *Shōjo Book*, courtesy of Shueisha Inc.
© "SHOJO BOOK" FIRST ISSUE/SHUEISHA Inc.

in which characters reveal their innermost feelings in monologues, establishing a sort of telepathic link with readers and eliciting empathy. Most importantly, young female readers closely identify with *shōjo* manga heroines because they see their own aspirations mirrored in these characters.

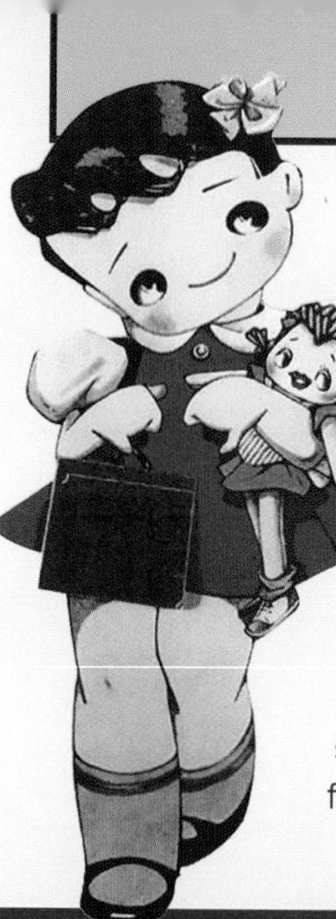

Artwork of *Kurukuru Kurumi-chan*, courtesy of the family of Katsuji Matsumoto

HISTORY OF *SHŌJO* MANGA

In 1928, Kitazawa Rakuten, the first professional *manga-ka* in Japan, published *Miss Haneko Tonda* (*Tonda Haneko-jō*) in *Jiji Manga*, a Sunday supplement to a newspaper. It was the first serialized manga in Japan featuring a young girl and is considered the prototype for modern *shōjo* manga. *Shōjo* magazines such as *Shōjo Club* (1923) first appeared before World War II, while others such as *Shōjo Book* (1951) launched afterwards. They contained mainly novels and illustrations but few manga. A pioneering *shōjo* manga was Katsuji Matsumoto's *Kurukuru Kurumi-chan* (1938). Japanese readers adored the manga, a trailblazer in the use of character-themed merchandise and an originator of *kawaii* (cute) culture.

Early *shōjo* manga were drawn mainly by male *manga-ka*. In 1953, Osamu Tezuka created *Princess Knight*, and the strength of its heroine, Princess Sapphire, inspired many female readers.

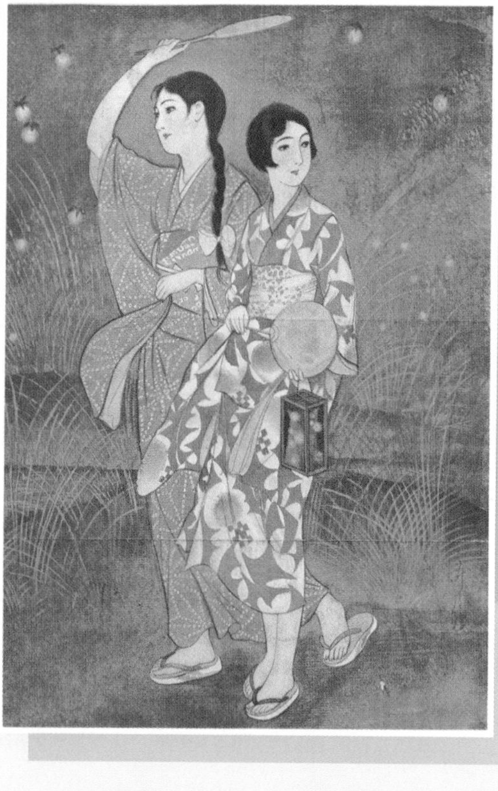

SO SUGOI!

Before World War II, close friendships between girls, known as Class S (*S kankei*), were popularized in magazines for girls. The letter *S* is an acronym for "sister" and refers to a sisterly friendship between two girls. *Shōjo* magazines published a series of "S" novels, and many girls established Class S friendships in their school lives, exchanging letters with one another. Even today, Class S is part of Japanese *shōjo* culture and continues to influence manga themes.

Seeing *Princess Knight*'s success, Kodansha, the publisher, understood there was a large target audience in young women, and in 1954 introduced the monthly girls' magazine *Nakayoshi*. The following year, *Ribon*, another major *shōjo* magazine, was launched by Shueisha. Eventually, some girls who grew up reading these manga became professional *shōjo manga-ka* themselves. Nowadays, *shōjo* manga are drawn mainly by women for younger female readers.

One of the first women to make her mark in manga was Hideko Mizuno (1939–). Not only was she the only female resident of Tokiwa-sō, Mizuno assisted Osamu Tezuka as well. She has a deep understanding of mythology, ballet, and opera. Besides fantastical stories based on those themes, Mizuno also writes gritty dramas that delve into the essence of human nature. A pioneer, Mizuno has profoundly influenced later generations of *manga-ka*.

Mizuno established herself as a manga artist with her work *Harp of the Stars* (*Hoshi no Tategoto*)—a love story

Above: Artwork of *Princess Knight*, courtesy of Tezuka Productions
© Tezuka Productions

Left: Self portrait of Hideko Mizuno
© Hideko Mizuno

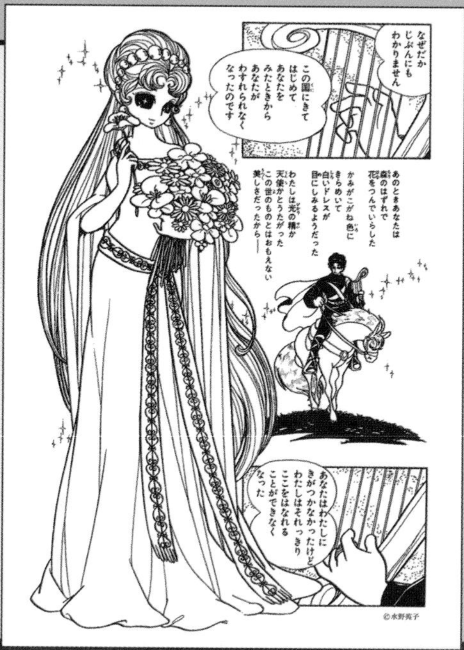
なぜだか
じぶんにも
わかりません
この国にきて
はじめて
あなたを
みたときから
あなたが
わすれられなく
なったのです
あのときあなたは
森のはずれで
花をつんでいらした
かみがこがね色に
きらめいて
白いドレスが
目にしみるようだった
わたしは光の精か
天使かとうたがった
この世のものとはおもえない
美しさだったから――
あなたはわたしに
きがつかなかったけど
わたしはそれっきり
ここをはなれる
ことができなく
なった
©水野英子

Artwork from *Harp of the Stars* (above) and cover of the first volume of *Harp of the Stars* (below), courtesy of Hideko Mizuno

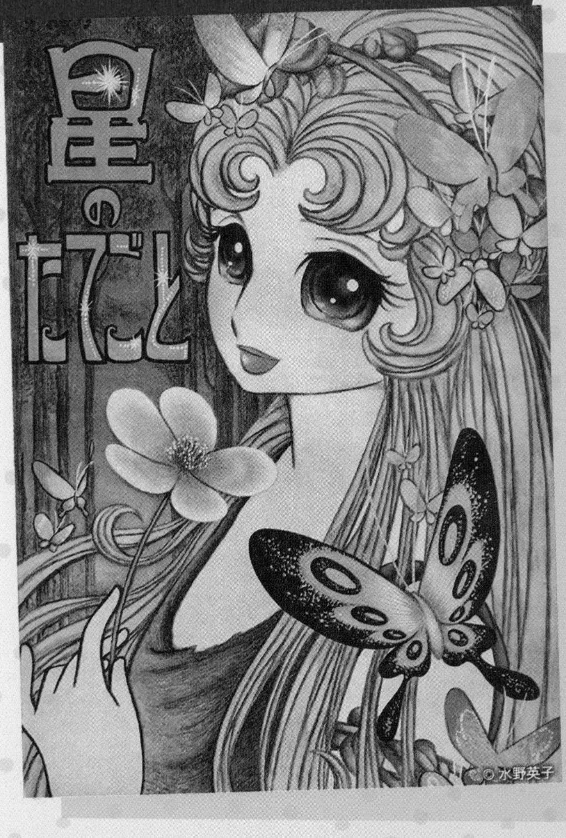
星のたてごと
©水野英子

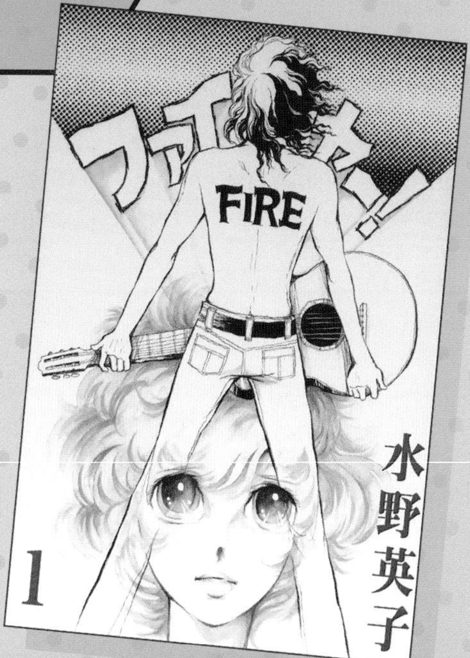
FIRE
水野英子
1

Cover of the first volume of *Fire!* (above) and artwork from *Fire!* (below), courtesy of Hideko Mizuno

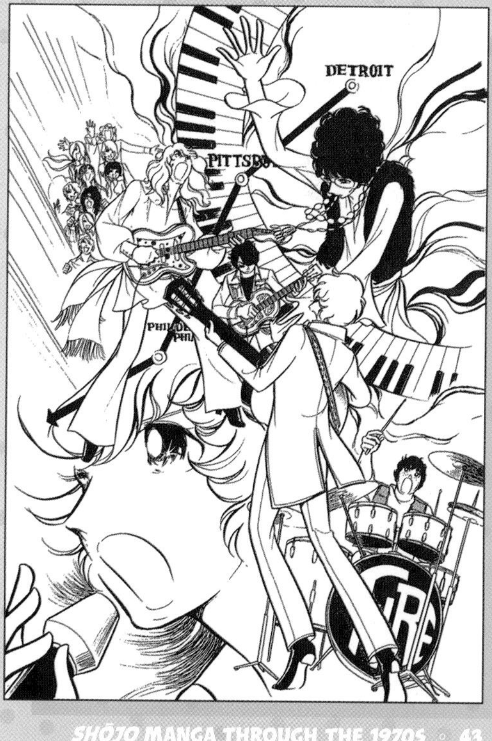
DETROIT

between a princess and a knight set in a fictional medieval world. She made her debut as a *manga-ka* in 1955 and published a series of highly narrative manga written from a woman's perspective. Mizuno is credited with laying the foundations for romance manga through her descriptive portrayals of male-female romances.

THE 1960S

The 1960s saw the debut of several innovative female *manga-ka*. They built on the manga created by male *manga-ka* and incorporated the trends of their time. One example is *Fire!* by Hideko Mizuno, a story set in the United States that portrays a boy who aspired to become a rock singer—it was notable that Mizuno made a male the main protagonist in a *shōjo* manga and that it was set in the United States. At the time, rock music conveyed a message of youth rebelling against society, and Mizuno incorporated this protest attitude into her manga. The expansive story line of *Fire!* made it a hit with both men and women.

The Tokyo Olympics in 1964 increased the popularity of *supokon* manga, the genre in which the main characters are devoted to sports. In 1968, two volleyball *shōjo* manga, *Attack No.1* and *The V Sign!*, were published in different magazines following the popularity of women's volleyball at the Olympics.

THE 1970S

The 1970s was the golden age of *shōjo* manga. The female *manga-ka* known as the Year 24 Group (*24 Nen Gumi*) reigned supreme during this decade. The Year 24 Group refers to *shōjo manga-ka* born around 1949 (the 24th year of the Shōwa era). They produced fantasy, science fiction, historical stories, and many dramatic *shōjo* manga. Girls and boys alike followed their work.

The dramas written by the Year 24 Group examined the characters' inner lives. Their innovative story lines upended previous perceptions of girls. Moto Hagio, known as "The Founding Mother of *Shōjo* Manga," is one of the leading *manga-ka* of the Year 24 Group. She has produced many influential works not restricted to the *shōjo* manga genre. Here are a few examples of the Year 24 Group's creations:

THE POE CLAN

(Pō no Ichizoku, 1972)

Western vampire legends inspired this masterpiece by Moto Hagio. It describes the story of Edgar, a vampire destined to live forever in a boy's body and what he loses by not growing up. The story influenced numerous manga-ka.

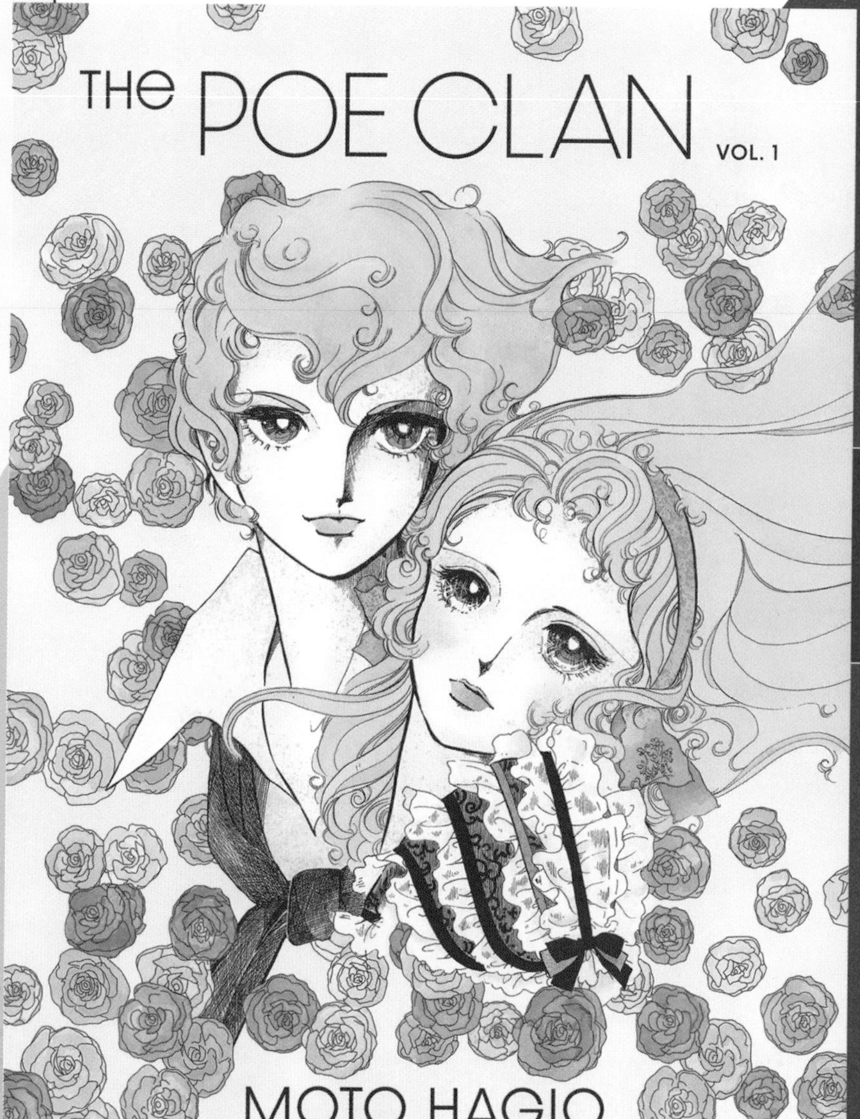

THE POE CLAN VOL. 1
MOTO HAGIO

Cover of the first Fantagraphics volume of *The Poe Clan*, courtesy of Fantagraphics Books

© Moto Hagio

THE POEM OF WIND AND TREES

(Kaze to Ki no Uta, 1976)

This tragic romance, created by Keiko Takemiya, is set in a 19th-century French school dormitory. In this dramatic tale, the main character, Gilbert, grew up without love but later opened his heart to Serge's devoted friendship.

COTTON'S COUNTRY STAR

(Wata no Kunihoshi, 1978)

This is a unique fantasy by Yumiko Ōshima about a little cat who wears a fluttery one-piece dress, an apron, and cat ears. The owner treats the cat like a pet, but the cat believes she will one day become human.

FROM EROICA WITH LOVE

(Eroica Yori Ai o Komete, 1976)

In this spy action comedy by Yasuko Aoike, Eroica, a beautiful blonde thief, and Iron Klaus, an army major employed by NATO military intelligence, collaborate and fight together to achieve their mutual goals in Europe.

エロイカより愛をこめて ①

青池保子

Cover of the first Japanese volume of *From Eroica With Love*.

During the 1970s, *shōjo* manga continued to diversify to meet readers' more varied tastes. Thanks to this group of talented female *manga-ka*, *shōjo* manga were no longer just for girls; college students and even adult men read the high-quality stories!

THE ROSE OF VERSAILLES

(*Berusaiyu no Bara*, 1972)

A work of historical fiction by Riyoko Ikeda, The Rose of Versailles *is set in France at the time of the French Revolution. It depicts the lives of Lady Oscar, who dresses as a man, and Marie Antoinette, Queen of France. The first half of the manga focuses on Lady Oscar and Marie Antoinette, then the action shifts to Oscar and the tragedy leading to the revolution. It was adapted for the stage by the Takarazuka Revue in 1974, followed by an animated TV series in 1979.*

ベルサイユのばら
the ROSE of VERSAILLES
RIYOKO IKEDA
UDON
1

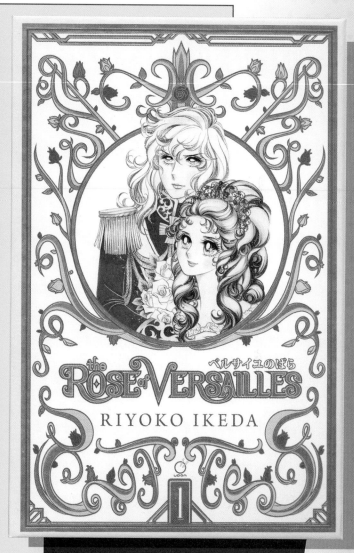

Cover of the first volume of *The Rose of Versailles*, courtesy of UDON Entertainment

AIM FOR THE ACE!

(Ēsu o Nerae!, 1973)

The story, created by Sumika Yamamoto, follows Hiromi Oka, who joins the high school tennis club and overcomes various hardships, including intense training and bullying by club members, to become a first-class tennis player. When it was serialized, this supokon manga sparked a tennis craze.

CANDY CANDY

(Kyandi Kyandi, 1975)

This series was created by Kyoko Mizuki and illustrated by Yumiko Igarashi. The story takes place in the United States and England in the early 20th century. It is the story of Candy, a bright and cheerful orphan girl who, while growing up, repeatedly meets and parts with people. There are many serious episodes that convey the feeling of separating from loved ones and the tragedy of war.

FUROKU

In 1977, *Chao* was launched by Shogakukan as a magazine for young girls in elementary school, joining *Nakayoshi* and *Ribon* as one of the three top *shōjo* manga magazines. *Furoku* (freebies) are a key factor in the popularity of *Chao*. *Furoku* are critical in getting young readers to pick up the magazine!

Furoku accompany magazines and cater to girls' dreams and longings. Until the 1990s, the most common types of *furoku* were stationery items, such as letter sets, notebooks, playing cards, and other paper crafts. In the 21st century, magazines started to include figurines of popular idols, which generated a huge sensation.

Today's *furoku* are even more luxurious; for example, a high-tech piggy bank whose contents cannot be accessed without inserting a card, or a palm-sized robot vacuum cleaner that automatically cleans your desk when turned on. It's hard to believe that the magazine *Chao* costs only about five dollars!

Examples of *furoku*

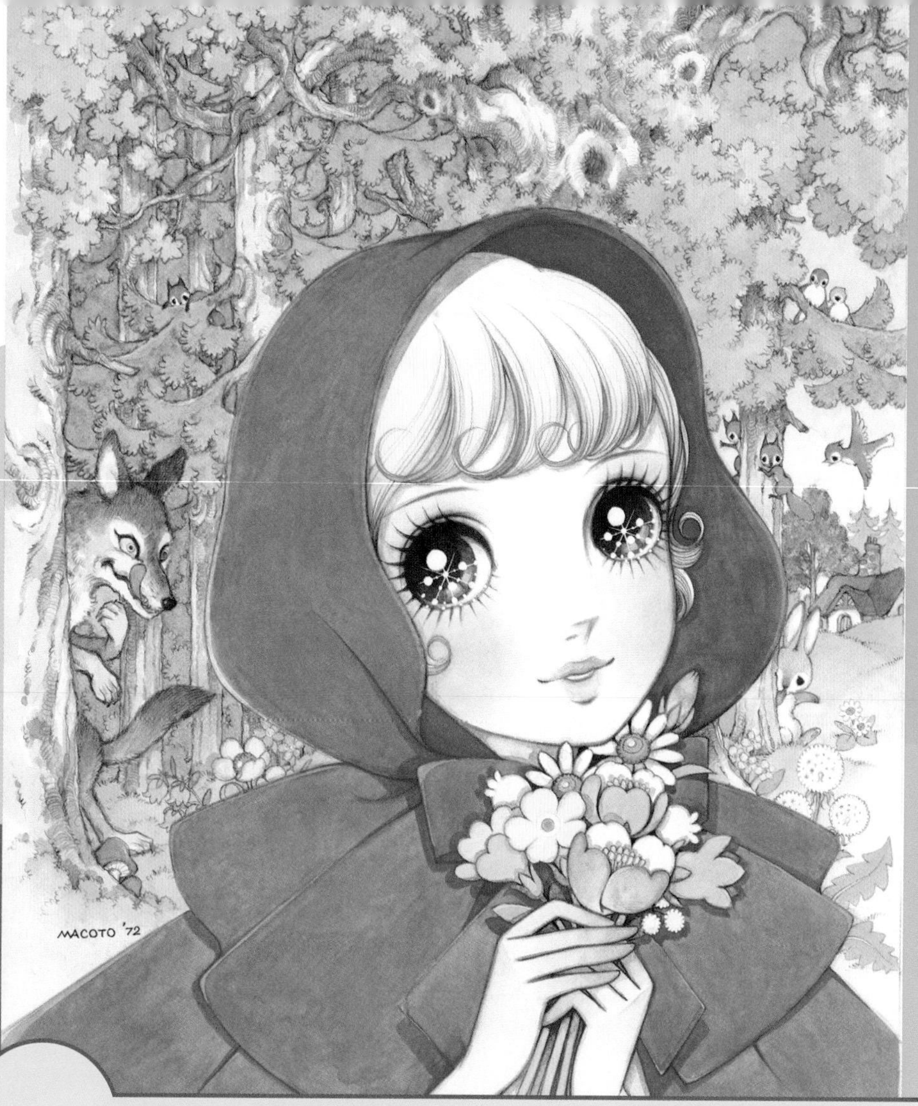
MACOTO '72

Little Red Riding Hood © Macoto Art

SO SUGOI!

Macoto Takahashi, an important figure in the early days of *shōjo* manga, illustrated fairy tales for little girls, including *The Little Mermaid*, *The Little Match Girl*, and *Snow White*, as well as many magazine and book cover illustrations.

Takahashi's style, in which flowers bloom all over the background, still carries on as a widely used *shōjo* manga technique today. One of his work's most distinctive features is seen in his characters' eyes. Takahashi perfected the style of placing sparkling stars in their eyes to express how passionately they devote themselves to their dreams. This technique of drawing large starry eyes profoundly influenced later *shōjo* manga.

MANGA THROUGH THE 1990S

1990年代までのマンガ

AKIRA TORIYAMA

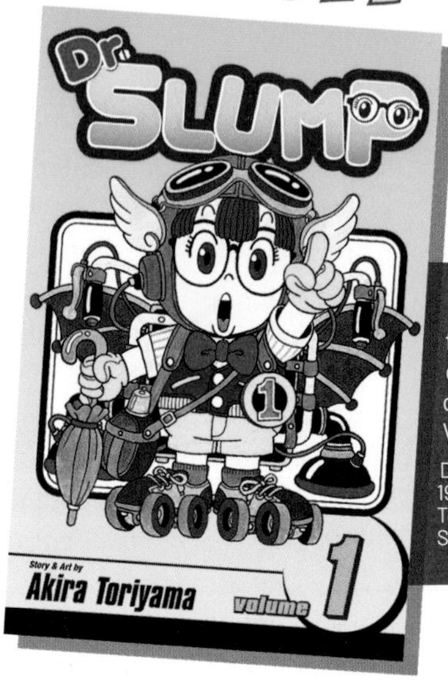
Dr. SLUMP
Story & Art by
Akira Toriyama
volume 1

Cover of the first volume of *Dr. Slump*, courtesy of VIZ Media

In 1980, *Weekly Shōnen Jump* began serializing *Dr. Slump*, the first big hit by the *manga-ka* Akira Toriyama. *Dr. Slump* starred the android Arale and was turned into a popular anime the following year. The manga was famous for its unique setting and worldview; many characters were animals, and Arale wore glasses despite being an android. Arale would say a variety of buzzwords that many children began to imitate, such as *n-cha* (hello) and *bai-cha* (good-bye).

If Akira Toriyama's name sounds familiar to you, it's because he's the creator of one of the most popular *shōnen* manga ever: *Dragon Ball*! Since 1984, the story of *Dragon Ball* has depicted the life of Son Goku from childhood to adulthood. Goku's son Gohan, his grandson Goten, and the friends Goku made during his adventures all play active roles as they face powerful enemies.

At the start of the series, *Dragon Ball* sometimes did not receive that much support from the readers' survey. However, once the story

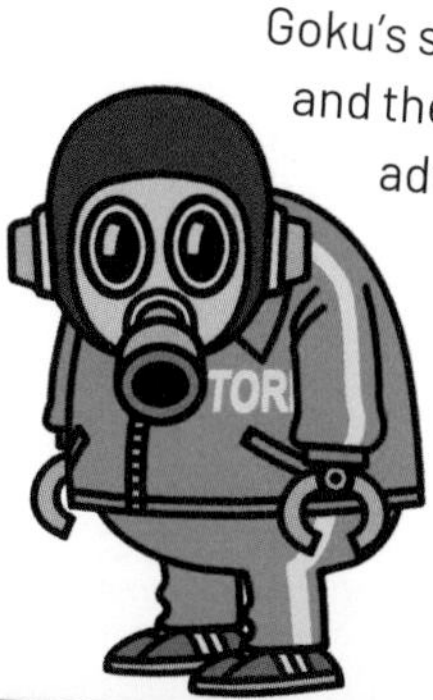
TOR

Self-portrait of Akira Toriyama

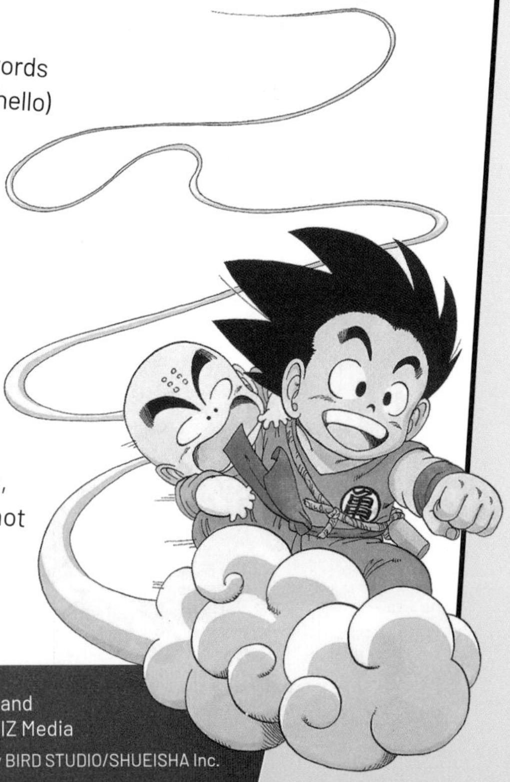

Artwork of Son Goku and Kuririn, courtesy of VIZ Media

changed its focus to battles, the series skyrocketed to the top of the charts and garnered worldwide appeal. *Dragon Ball* was later adapted into a TV anime series and still inspires movie versions—the latest released in 2022.

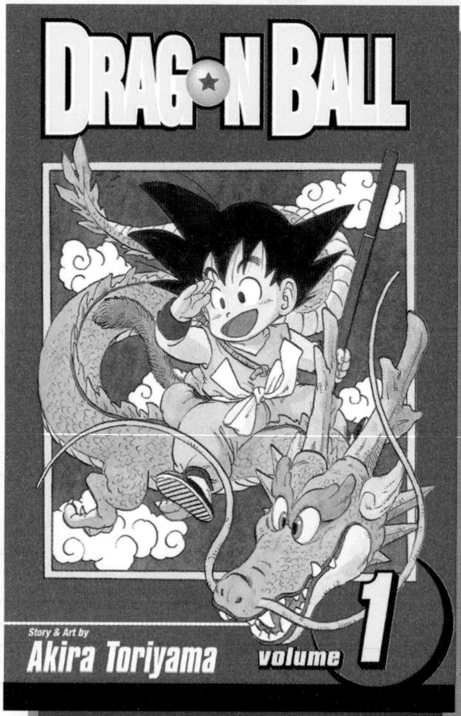
DRAGON BALL
Story & Art by
Akira Toriyama
volume 1

Cover of the first volume of *Dragon Ball*, courtesy of VIZ Media

DRAGON BALL © 1984 by BIRD STUDIO/ SHUEISHA Inc.

RUMIKO TAKAHASHI

Rumiko Takahashi, one of the masters of romantic comedy, serialized her first popular *shōnen* manga work, *Urusei Yatsura*, in 1978 while she was still a university student. This romantic comedy involves Ataru, a high school student who always chases girls, and Lum, a girl from outer space. The anime series became very popular in the 1980s, and in 2022, a new version of the anime series was produced to commemorate the 100th anniversary of the founding of Shogakukan, the publisher of *Weekly Shōnen Sunday.*

For a young author to achieve even one manga hit is remarkable, but Takahashi had an extraordinary number of hits after *Urusei Yatsura*, including long-running series adapted into anime. Some of Takahashi's most popular *shōnen* manga include *Ranma ½* (1987) and *Inuyasha* (1996).

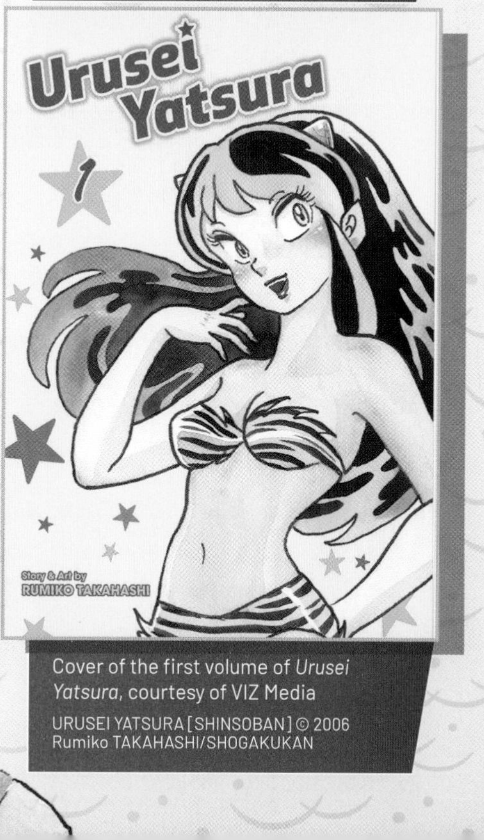
Urusei Yatsura
1
Story & Art by
RUMIKO TAKAHASHI

Cover of the first volume of *Urusei Yatsura*, courtesy of VIZ Media

URUSEI YATSURA [SHINSOBAN] © 2006 Rumiko TAKAHASHI/SHOGAKUKAN

Ranma ½ is a romantic comedy about a high school boy named Ranma. When covered in cold water, Ranma becomes a girl but returns to being a boy when dowsed in hot water. The naïve interactions between Ranma and Akane swelled readers' hearts with excitement.

Inuyasha takes place during the Warring States period in Japan's history. The story tells of a romance between Inuyasha, a half demon, and Kagome, a girl who

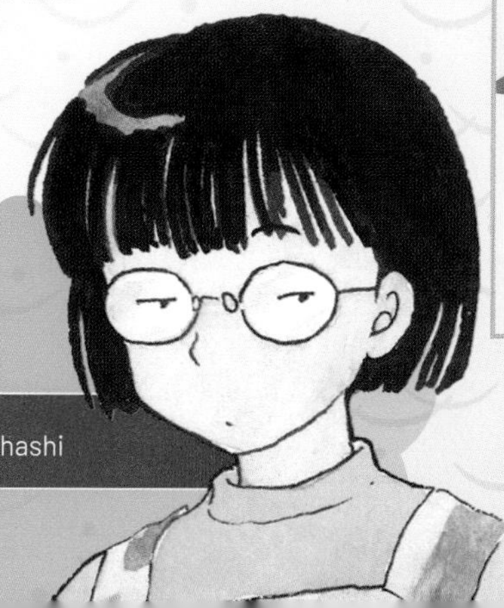

Self-portrait of Rumiko Takahashi

slipped back in time. *Inuyasha* is less comedic than some of Takahashi's other works, the focus being the defeat of the enemy Naraku.

Takahashi was inducted into the Harvey Awards Hall of Fame in 2021, one of the most prestigious awards in the US comics industry. Osamu Tezuka was the first Japanese *manga-ka* inducted into this Hall of Fame in 2020.

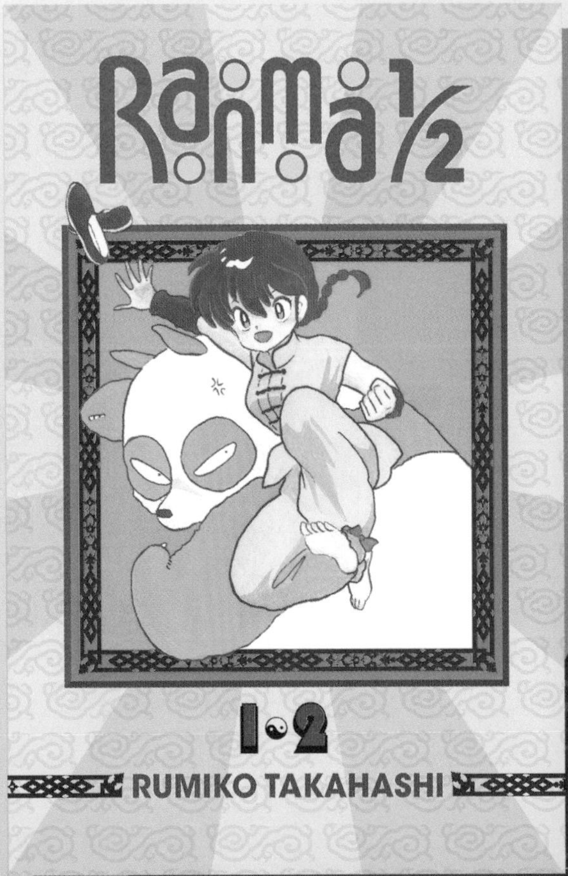
Ranma 1/2
1·2
RUMIKO TAKAHASHI

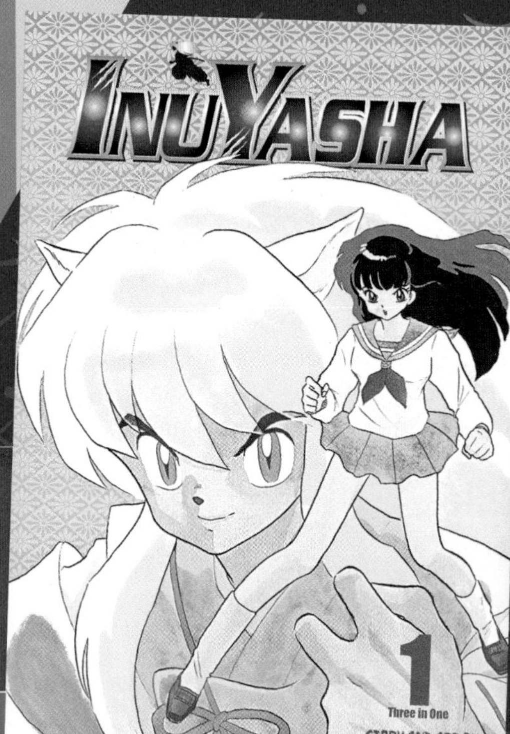
INUYASHA
1
Three in One
SHONEN SUNDAY MANGA
STORY AND ART BY
RUMIKO TAKAHASHI

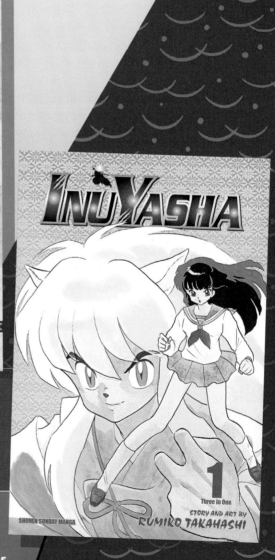

Above: Cover of the first volume of *Ranma 1/2*, courtesy of VIZ Media

Right: Cover of the first volume of *Inuyasha*, courtesy of VIZ Media

POPULAR *SHŌNEN* MANGA OF THE 1980S

CAPTAIN TSUBASA

(*Kyaputen Tsubasa*, 1981)

Created by Yoichi Takahashi, this is the story of Tsubasa Ozora, who loves soccer and whose motto is "the soccer ball is my friend." The manga was extremely popular among men and women and influenced by the soccer boom in society. The series was still running in 2022, and Tsubasa and his friends, who were initially elementary school students, are now working as professional athletes in various countries.

Cover of the first volume of *Captain Tsubasa*, courtesy of Shueisha Inc.

CAPTAIN TSUBASA © 1981 by Yoichi Takahashi/SHUEISHA Inc.

JOJO'S BIZARRE ADVENTURE

(*JoJo no Kimyō na Bōken*, 1986)

In this unique manga created by Hirohiko Araki, the main character changes in each series, but they are all nicknamed JoJo and are all descended from Sir George Joestar, an English nobleman. JoJo is famous for its distinctive characters, none of whom, enemy or ally, are ordinary!

Cover of the first volume of *JoJo's Bizarre Adventure*, courtesy of VIZ Media

JOJO'S BIZARRE ADVENTURE © 1986 by Hirohiko Araki/SHUEISHA Inc.

SHŌJO MANGA OF THE 1980S

In the 1980s, a subgenre of *shōjo* called *otome-chikku* (girly) manga became popular. It was based on girlish school activities, featuring a shift in the story setting from fantasy to everyday life. Rather than a super-talented girl, the heroine was an ordinary schoolgirl, and the hero was no longer a charming prince but an ordinary boy at the same school.

In the late 1980s, the serialization of the hit comedy manga *Chibi Maruko-chan* started up. *Shōjo* manga did not initially have as many gags as *shōnen* manga, but in this story, romance wasn't the top draw, and it proved that a *shōjo* manga could become a megahit without a romantic story line!

POPULAR *SHŌJO* MANGA OF THE 1980S

YŪKAN CLUB
(*Yūkan Kurabu*, 1981)

Created by Yukari Ichijō, Yūkan Club follows six main characters, all members of a student council, as they use their unique talents, knowledge, and connections to guide them through various situations ranging from romantic encounters to political drama and even the occult. Each character has a different personality and sense of values, but they are all humane and righteous people angered by evil and absurdity in the world.

CHIBI MARUKO-CHAN
(1986)

Set in the town where she was born, the author, Momoko Sakura, recounts the sometimes funny, sometimes sad memories of her childhood in this manga. The manga surreally and comically depicts the daily events of the goofy Maruko, her charming family, and her unique classmates.

Cover of the first volume of *Chibi Maruko-chan*, courtesy of Shueisha Inc.

CHIBI MARUKO-CHAN © 1986 by Sakura Production Co., Ltd./ SHUEISHA Inc.

POPULAR *SHŌNEN* MANGA OF THE 1990S

Known as the "Golden Age of *Shōnen Jump*," the 1990s saw a string of hits based on the magazine's concepts of friendship, effort, and victory. Here are a few of the best-known works, some of which are still popular today, both in Japan and internationally.

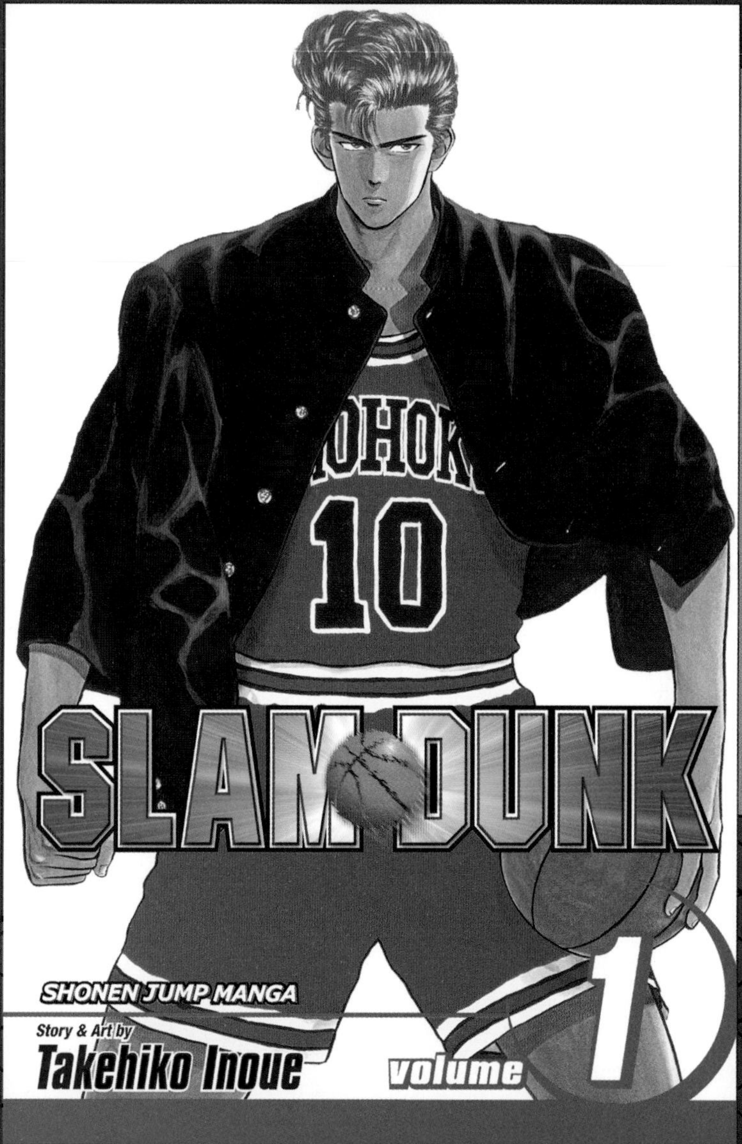
SLAM DUNK
SHONEN JUMP MANGA
Story & Art by
Takehiko Inoue
volume 1

SLAM DUNK

(1990)

In this manga created by Takehiko Inoue, Hanamichi Sakuragi, a high school delinquent, joins the basketball club on the advice of Haruko, with whom he falls in love at first sight. Hanamichi, a novice player despite his talent, surprisingly evolves as a basketball player. With his exceptional skills, he strives to capture the national championship alongside his teammates.

Cover of the first volume of *Slam Dunk*, courtesy of VIZ Media

RUROUNI KENSHIN

(*Rurōni Kenshin*, 1994)

Nobuhiro Watsuki created this story of the legendary swordsman Kenshin, feared as "Hitokiri Battōsai" at the end of the Tokugawa shogunate (the military government of Japan from the 17th to 19th centuries). He swore never to kill again after the shogunate ended, and continued his journey as a wanderer helping others.

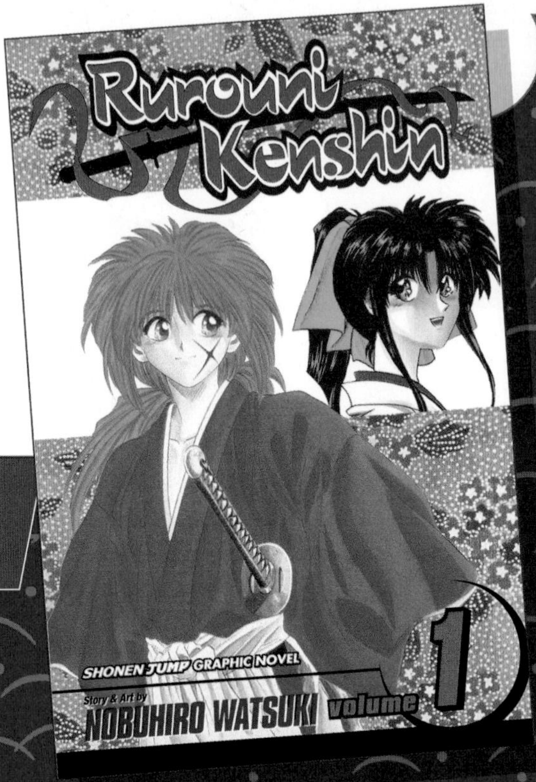
Rurouni Kenshin
SHONEN JUMP GRAPHIC NOVEL
Story & Art by
NOBUHIRO WATSUKI
volume 1

Cover of the first volume of *Rurouni Kenshin*, courtesy of VIZ Media

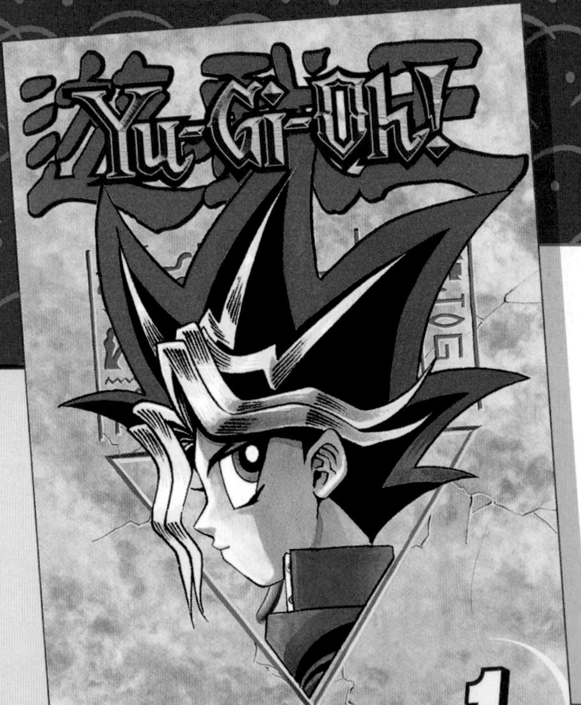
Yu-Gi-Oh!
SHONENJUMP MANGA
Story & Art by
Kazuki Takahashi
volume 1

YU-GI-OH!

(*Yū-Gi-Ō!*, 1996)

Created by Kazuki Takahashi, Yugi, a high school student who loves video games, completes a puzzle that originated in ancient Egypt called the Millennium Puzzle. As a result, he is inhabited by another persona, Yami (Dark) Yugi. He plays a variety of games against opponents and unravels the mysteries of the Millennium Puzzle.

Cover of the first volume of *Yu-Gi-Oh!*, courtesy of VIZ Media

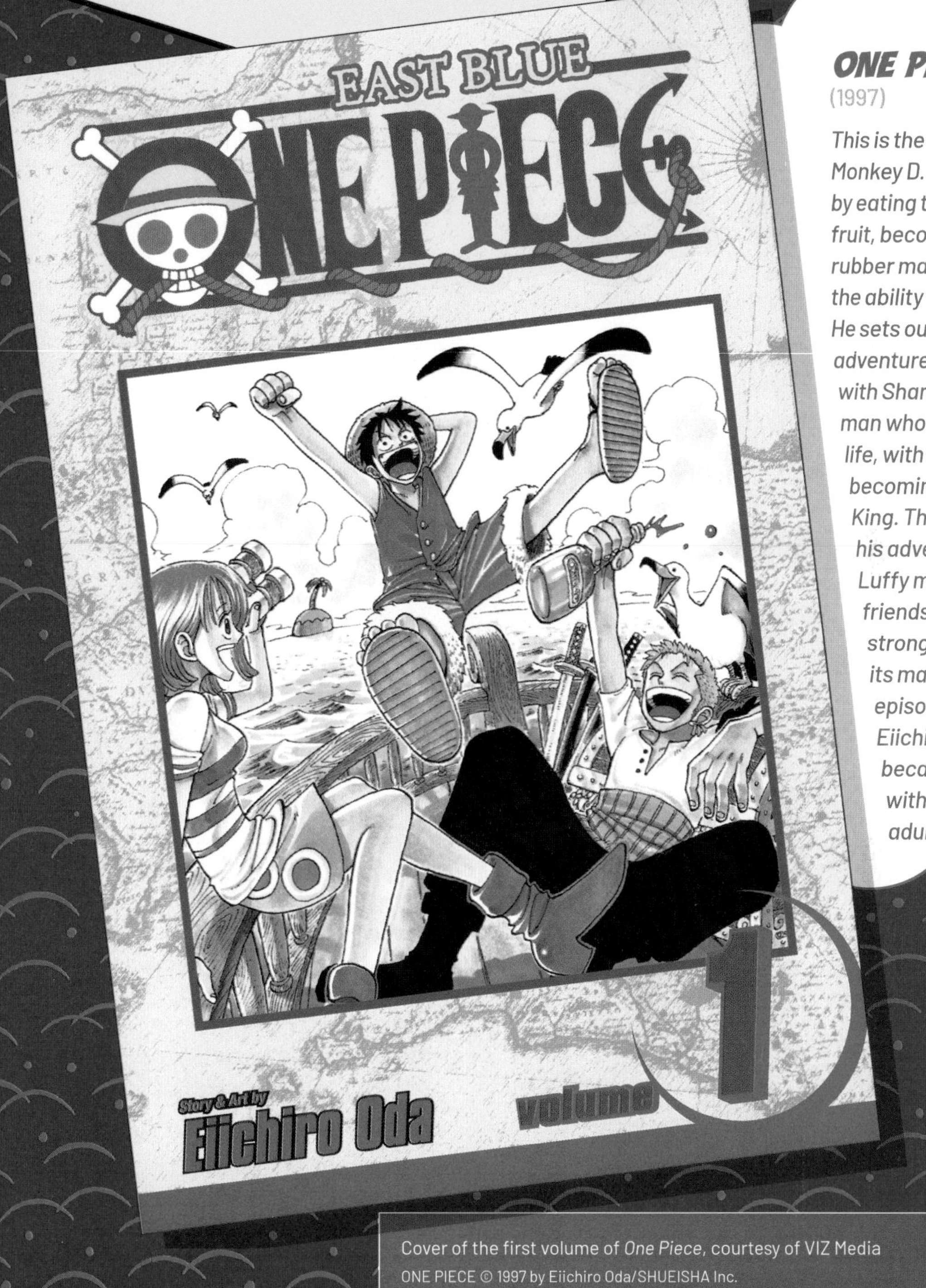
EAST BLUE
ONE PIECE
Story & Art by
Eiichiro Oda
volume
1

Cover of the first volume of *One Piece*, courtesy of VIZ Media

ONE PIECE

(1997)

This is the story of Monkey D. Luffy, who, by eating the devil's fruit, becomes a rubber man but loses the ability to swim. He sets out on an adventure to reunite with Shanks, the man who saved his life, with the goal of becoming the Pirate King. Throughout his adventures, Luffy makes many friends and grows stronger. With its many moving episodes, this Eiichiro Oda work became popular with children and adults alike.

SO SUGOI!

The 103rd volume of *One Piece* was released in August 2022. Five hundred million copies of the comic book series have been printed worldwide, all written by one person! *One Piece* surpasses all the Batman comics combined and is only the second literary work to exceed 500 million copies, the other being Harry Potter.

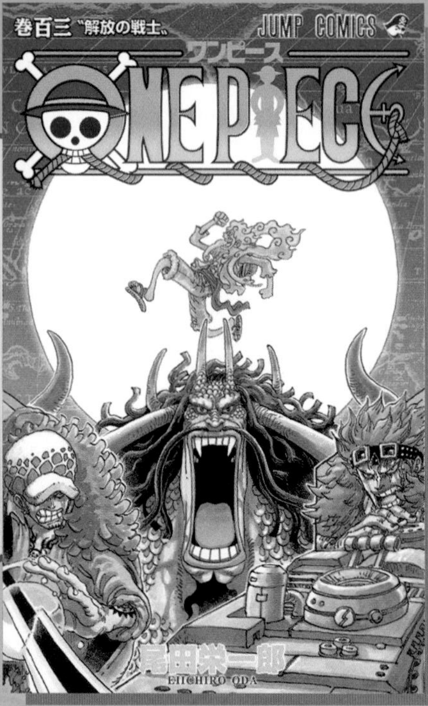

巻百三 "解放の戦士"
JUMP COMICS
ワンピース
ONE PIECE
尾田栄一郎
EIICHIRO ODA

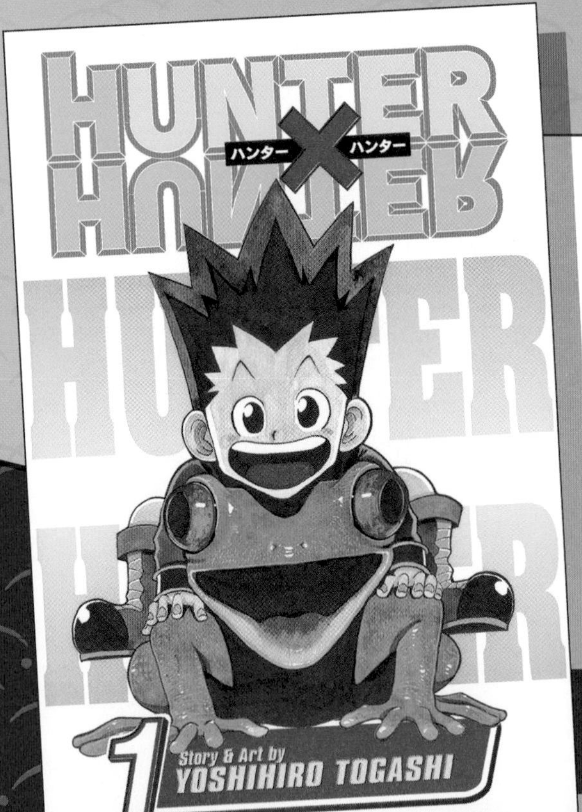

HUNTER × HUNTER
ハンター ハンター
1
Story & Art by
YOSHIHIRO TOGASHI

HUNTER × HUNTER

(1998)

The main character, Gon Freecss, becomes a hunter and searches for his father while experiencing a series of adventures with friends. Although the themes relate to the protagonist's growth and friendships, the story is characterized by a dark worldview. Its carefully planned settings and foreshadowing mood made it quite popular.

Cover of the first volume of *Hunter × Hunter*, courtesy of VIZ Media

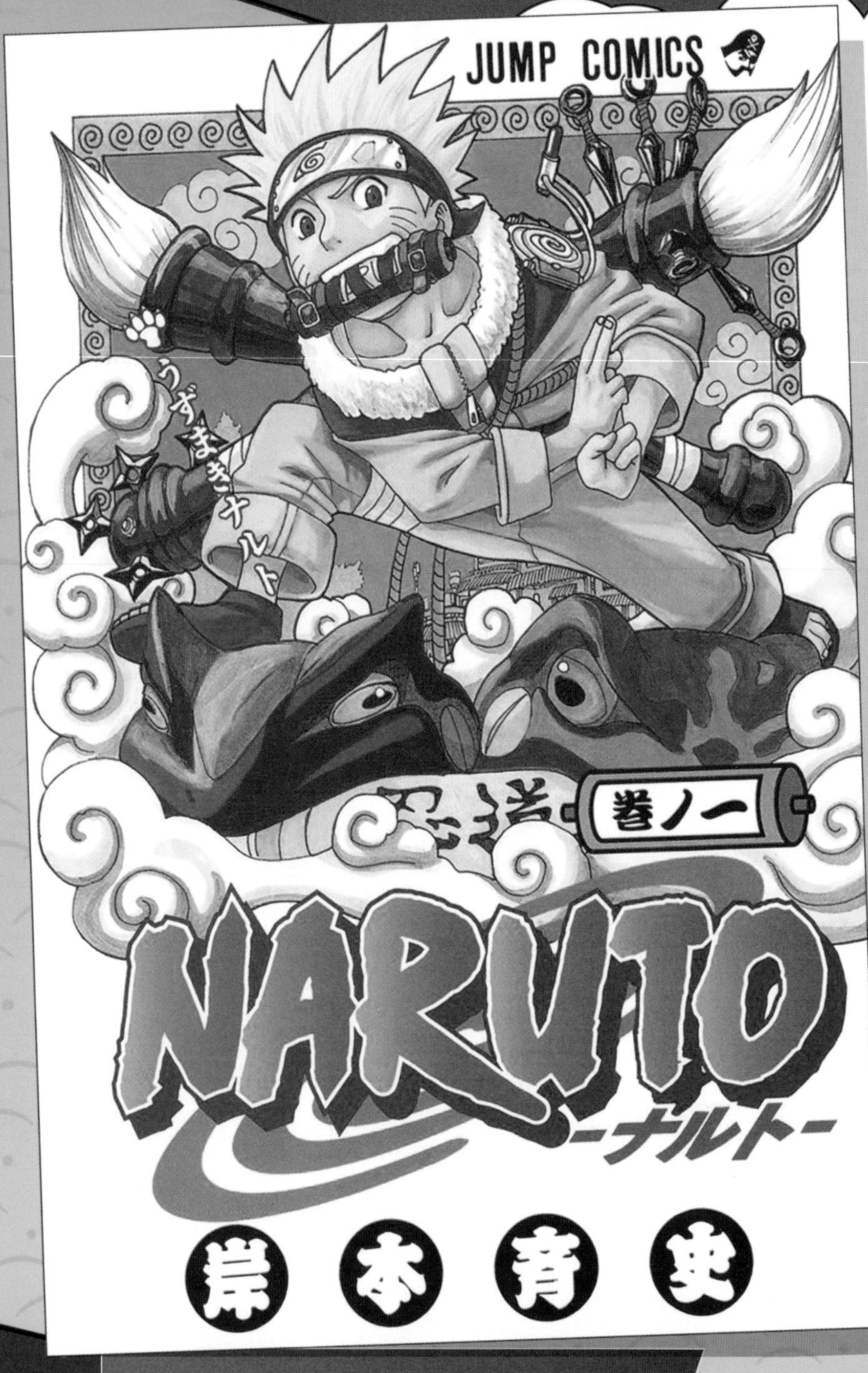
JUMP COMICS
うずまきナルト
巻ノ一
NARUTO
-ナルト-
岸本斉史

Cover of the first volume of *Naruto*, courtesy of VIZ Media

NARUTO

(1999)

Created by Masashi Kishimoto, the story depicts the coming-of-age of dropout ninja Uzumaki Naruto and his friendships as he struggles against powerful enemies. The manga is recognized for the development and humanity of the characters' personalities, the story's structure, and the fantastic depiction of ninja techniques. A sequel manga, Boruto: Naruto Next Generations, *was also serialized.*

SHŌJO MANGA OF THE 1990S

Fighting heroines became a popular element of *shōjo* manga in the 1990s. The idea of the passive heroine was put to rest and replaced by the concept of the independent-minded woman who sets out on her own to seek happiness. This was a profound change that garnered the support of many young female readers. One possible reason was Japan's 1985 Equal Employment Opportunity Law, in which women gained more rights and elevated societal status. The globally popular *Sailor Moon* is an excellent example of a fighting heroine manga.

Also, the 1990s saw an increase in manga tackling emotional and psychological issues. In *Iguana Girl*, Moto Hagio portrays a mother who cannot love her daughter. The story was such a hit that it was adapted into a live-action drama. Dramas based on manga had been aired in the past but were mainly lighthearted romances; *Iguana Girl* was in a class by itself.

The 1990s was also a period of growth for *josei* (women's) manga, which targeted adult women. The *josei* manga were well received by women struggling with work and adult romance and successfully captured the spirit of a generation that had moved beyond the *shōjo* manga directed at young girls.

SAILOR MOON
(*Bishōjo Senshi Sērā Mūn*, 1991)

This work by Naoko Takeuchi is popular all over the world! Usagi is an ordinary second-year junior high school student who is a bit clumsy and whiny. One day, Usagi meets a mysterious black cat named Luna with a crescent moon on its forehead. Luna gives Usagi a magical brooch that transforms her into Sailor Moon, a warrior destined to fight evil forces.

BOYS *over* FLOWERS

Hana Yori Dango

FLOWERS

1

STORY AND ART BY **YOKO KAMIO**

BOYS OVER FLOWERS
(Hana yori Dango, 1992)

The story, created by Yoko Kamio, concerns the struggles of a poor girl, Tsukushi, who enters a school with many wealthy students. It has some serious elements, such as discrimination and bullying, but is also a gag comedy about Tsukushi and the F4, a group of rich, handsome boys.

Cover of the first volume of *Boys Over Flowers*, courtesy of VIZ Media

IGUANA GIRL
(Iguana no Musume, 1992)

This Moto Hagio work depicts
the conflict between Rika
and her mother, who cannot
love Rika because, in her
imagination, she sees Rika as
an ugly iguana. The anguish of
both is depicted with elements
of fantasy. Rika also begins
to see herself in the mirror
as an iguana, which makes
her believe she will not have a
bright future.

Cover of *Iguana Girl* (left) and panel
from *Iguana Girl* (below), courtesy
of Fantagraphic Books
Copyright © Moto Hagio

YOU
HATE ME
BECAUSE
I'M AN
IGUANA!

CARDCAPTOR SAKURA

(*Kādokyaputā Sakura*, 1996)

This is a popular work by CLAMP, a group of four female manga-ka. A fourth-grade elementary school student, Sakura, discovers a mysterious book in her father's library. In the book, she finds a Clow Card that will bring misfortune to the world. Sakura becomes a Cardcaptor and battles to retrieve the Clow Cards unleashed on the planet.

COLLECTOR'S EDITION
Fruits Basket
NATSUKI TAKAYA
1

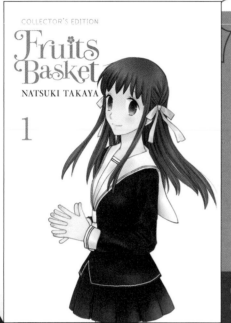

FRUITS BASKET

(*Furūtsu Basuketto*, 1998)

This manga, created by Natsuki Takaya, tells the story of Tohru Honda. After an unfortunate family tragedy turns Tohru into an orphan, she moves into a tent on private land belonging to the mysterious Sohma family. It doesn't take long before the owners discover Tohru's secret and take her in, but they have a shocking family secret of their own! In helping the Sohma family with their hardships, Tohru also learns more about herself and how much others care about her.

Cover of the first volume of *Fruits Basket*, courtesy of Yen Press

SO SUGOI!

Treating fictional characters as if they were actually alive may be unique to the Japanese. When famous characters such as Raoh from *Fist of the North Star* (*Hokuto no Ken*, 1983) or Tōru Rikiishi from the renowned boxing manga *Tomorrow's Joe* (*Ashita no Joe*, 1968) died in their stories, Japanese fans held real-life funerals! The social behavior of holding funerals for manga and anime characters is unique.

Their reaction could be attributed to Shinto, an ancient Japanese religion that holds that all things on earth are inhabited by deities—a fundamental concept in Japanese society and culture, even today. This Shinto belief system may explain the readers' spiritual intuition that fictional characters possess an element of life.

MANGA IN THE 21ST CENTURY
マンガの21世紀

1 n the 2000s, the internet brought manga to many readers, and technological advancements led to alternate ways of reading manga. This surge in readership ushered in new manga genres and trends to entertain newcomers.

During this time, manga for adults took priority over manga for children due to Japan's declining birth rate. Manga from this era tended to be thought-provoking and became popular with both men and women. For example, *NANA*, serialized beginning in 2000, is a *shōjo* manga but is adult-oriented. It sensitively portrays the loves, dreams, and conflicts of young adults.

Meanwhile, with the spread of smartphones, manga apps also grew in popularity. Earlier manga were serialized only in magazines such as *Weekly Shōnen Jump*, but from the 2000s on, more and more manga were published through smartphone apps.

Although there is an increasing variety of manga genres and new ways to enjoy manga, the overriding goal of manga—to entertain readers—remains unchanged!

In a way, manga form a historical record by capturing the lifestyles of the eras in which they are published. They reflect changes in things like fashion, architecture, and technology. For example, if you read Osamu Tezuka's works chronologically, you will learn about Japan's society, economy, postwar technological development, and period of rapid economic growth. Even if you read old manga just for enjoyment, you will get a lesson in Japanese culture and history as an add-on.

POPULAR *SHŌNEN* MANGA OF THE 21ST CENTURY

FULLMETAL ALCHEMIST

(*Hagane no Renkinjutsushi*, 2001)

This is a dark fantasy created by Hiromu Arakawa about two alchemist brothers, Edward and Alphonse Elric. Using alchemy, they attempt to bring their mother back to life after she died in an epidemic but fail. Edward loses an arm and a leg, and Alphonse loses his body—his remaining soul is encased in armor. The brothers travel in search of the Philosopher's Stone to regain what they have lost.

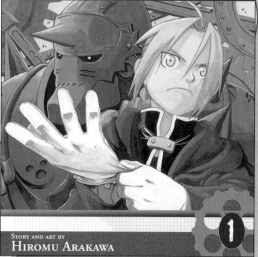

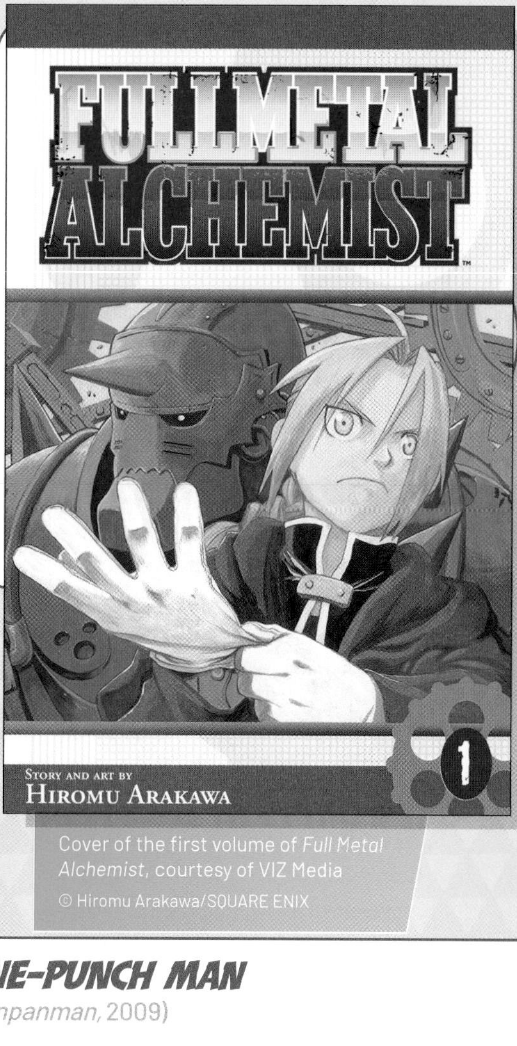

FULLMETAL ALCHEMIST
™
1
Story and art by
Hiromu Arakawa

Cover of the first volume of *Full Metal Alchemist*, courtesy of VIZ Media

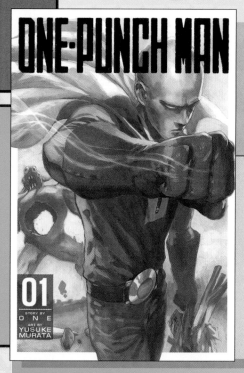

ONE-PUNCH MAN

(*Wanpanman*, 2009)

One-Punch Man *was originally a web manga created by ONE, but it began serializing with art by Yusuke Murata in* Tonari no Young Jump *in 2012. To pursue his dream of becoming a hero, young Saitama trains so hard for three years that he loses his hair and acquires the power to defeat his enemies with a single punch. However, because he beats his foes so easily, Saitama eventually gets bored, becoming an indifferent hero!*

ONE-PUNCH MAN
01
STORY BY
ONE
ART BY
YUSUKE
MURATA

Cover of the first volume of *One-Punch Man*, courtesy of VIZ Media

HAIKYU!!
(*Haikyū!!*, 2012)

Haruichi Furudate created this sports manga about high school volleyball. It is the story of the Karasuno High School volleyball club, centered around the two main characters, Shoyo Hinata and Tobio Kageyama, who mature as they take on powerful schools in their quest to win the national championship. Haikyū means volleyball in Japanese.

Cover of the first volume of *Haikyu!!*, courtesy of VIZ Media
HAIKYU!! © 2012 by Haruichi Furudate/SHUEISHA Inc.

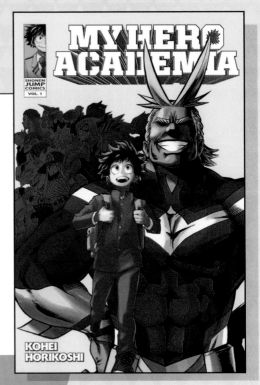

MY HERO ACADEMIA
(*Boku no Hīrō Akademia*, 2014)

Set in a world where about 80 percent of the population has a Quirk, or superpower, Izuku Midoriya is born without one. However, after rescuing a bully, Izuku inherits a Quirk from his childhood idol and is accepted into U.A. High School for hero training. This manga, created by Kohei Horikoshi, depicts the battles, friendships, and coming-of-age of Izuku and his classmates as they develop into heroes who protect society.

Cover of the first volume of *My Hero Academia*, courtesy of VIZ Media
BOKU NO HERO ACADEMIA © 2014 by Kohei Horikoshi/SHUEISHA Inc.

DEMON SLAYER: KIMETSU NO YAIBA

(2016)

After a demon slays his family, Tanjiro Kamado searches for a way to turn his young sister, Nezuko, who was transformed into a demon, back into a human. Eventually, Tanjiro becomes a member of the Demon Slayer Corps and joins battles to protect people. Koyoharu Gotouge's dark fantasy manga depicts Tanjiro's confrontations with demons and his growth as an individual.

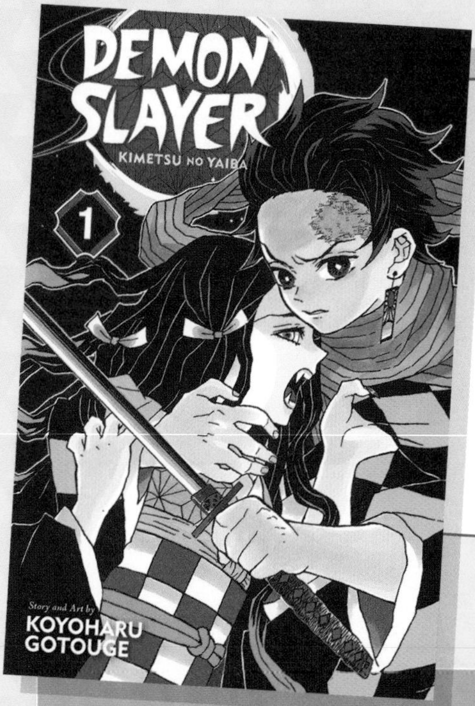
DEMON SLAYER
KIMETSU NO YAIBA
1
Story and Art by
KOYOHARU GOTOUGE

Cover of the first volume of *Demon Slayer: Kimetsu no Yaiba*, courtesy of VIZ Media

SPY×FAMILY

(2019)

This action home comedy tells the story of the psychic girl Anya, the male spy Loid, and the beautiful assassin Yor, who live together as a temporary family. Tatsuya Endo's heartwarming tale of three strangers, who don't know one another's true identities but gradually become a real family, plays out in full comedic style.

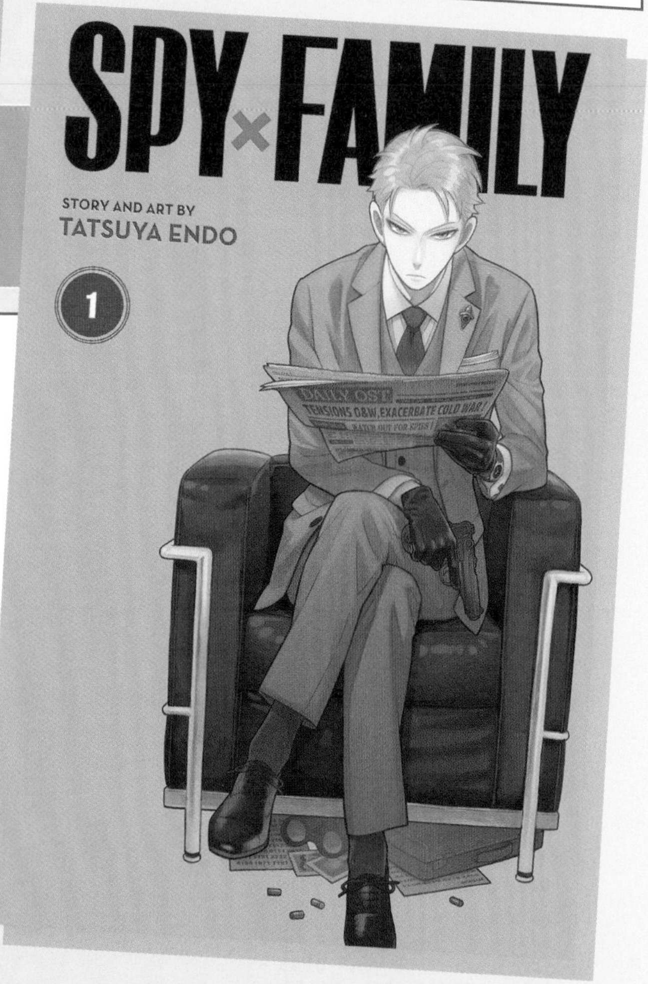
SPY×FAMILY
STORY AND ART BY
TATSUYA ENDO
1
DAILY OSE
TENSIONS O&W, EXACERBATE COLD WAR!
WATCH OUT FOR SPIES!

Cover of the first volume of *SPY x Family*, courtesy of VIZ Media

During the 2000s, *shōjo* manga diversified by exploring themes other than romance. This new direction displayed the shifting lifestyles of women choosing higher education and full-time careers over the role of homemaker. As more women stayed in the workforce, even after marriage, cliché concepts such as "marriage is a woman's happiness" have slowly melted away. More women wanted lifestyles that would allow them to express their individuality. To address these women's interests, the *shōjo* manga of the 2000s explored themes such as friendship and career paths, as well as other issues like child-rearing, gender discrimination, and aging.

POPULAR *SHŌJO* MANGA OF THE 21ST CENTURY

NANA

(1999)

The main characters are Nana Komatsu, who grew up in an ordinary family with no particular ambitions in life, and cool Nana Osaki, who was abandoned by her parents as a child and yearns for success in a band. These two contrasting Nanas in their 20s meet by chance on a bullet train heading to Tokyo and soon after move in together. Created by Ai Yazawa, the story revolves around the Nanas' relationship and their polar-opposite personalities.

Shojo Beat Manga

NANA

Story & Art by
Ai Yazawa

Cover of the first volume of *NANA*, courtesy of VIZ Media

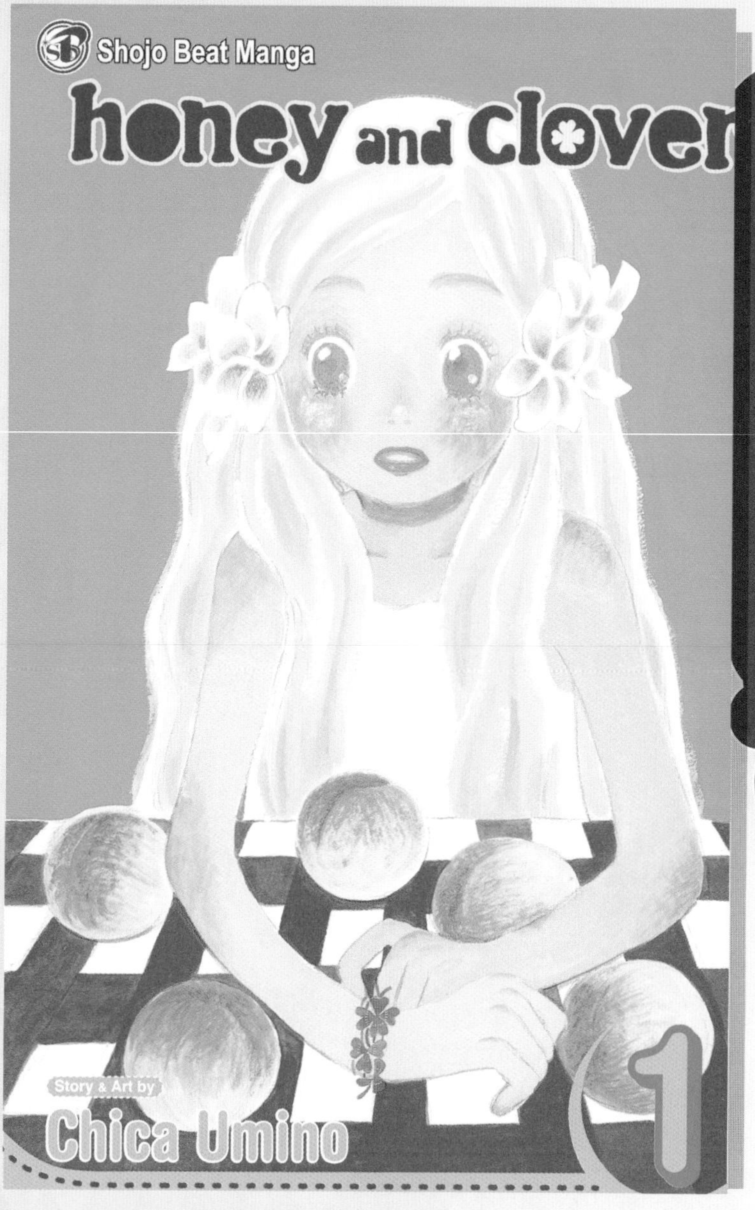
Shojo Beat Manga
honey and clover
1
Story & Art by
Chica Umino

HONEY AND CLOVER

(*Hachimitsu to Kurōbā*, 2000)

This story, created by Chica Umino, is set at an art college and skillfully shows the importance of pursuing one's dreams. The story line explores a stifling romance and the difficulties young adults face as they set out on a career path. It is popularly known by the abbreviation Hachikuro.

Cover of the first volume of *Honey and Clover*, courtesy of VIZ Media

NODAME CANTABILE

(*Nodame Kantābire*, 2001)

Nodame Cantabile *is a classical music-oriented comedy manga created by Tomoko Ninomiya about two talented young musicians: the free-spirited Megumi and the perfectionist Shinichi. The two are drawn to each other's talents and engage in friendly competition. Through their encounters and experiences with various people, they mature as individuals.*

CAREERS IN MANGA
マンガ業界

1 f you dream of working in manga, why not make that dream a reality! Even if you are not confident about writing and drawing, there are many important jobs in the industry that utilize other skills. If your passion is shaping stories and characters or translating manga to make them available to non-Japanese readers, there is a career in manga for you!

MANGA-KA

If your heart is set on becoming a *manga-ka*, it certainly helps to be an amazing writer and/or illustrator, but it takes a lot more to achieve success. *Manga-ka* must create unique and imaginative stories and characters that captivate their readers. Their ability to express characters' emotions through drawings and have readers empathize with them is just as important. Creating manga is hard work. *Manga-ka* need to stay focused and maintain mental and physical strength to meet deadlines.

There are many paths to becoming a *manga-ka*. One path open to beginners is to apply for manga prizes, which major publishers award during the year. Another is to submit work to a publishing company directly. Others enter the profession by connecting with editors while working as assistants to established *manga-ka*. More recently, another option is to attend a manga technical school and acquire the necessary skills in a classroom setting.

Today, manga plays a prominent role in Japanese pop culture. As more talented *manga-ka* join the field, readers of all orientations and ages find genres to choose from. In recent years, with the development of the internet, digital publishing has enabled *manga-ka* to directly reach readers online. Like self-promoting YouTubers, these *manga-ka* can bypass traditional publishers and post their work online at a minimal cost. Once a work becomes popular, it can be adapted into an anime, live-action drama, movie, or even a video game!

INTERVIEW
MANGA-KA *NATSUKI TAKAYA*

Self-portrait of
Natsuki Takaya

Manga-ka Natsuki Takaya was born and raised in Tokyo, Japan.
Ever since she was in first grade, she wanted to be a *manga-ka*,
and in 1992 her dream came true when "Born Free" debuted in
Hana to Yume Planet Zōkan magazine.

In 1998, Natsuki's *Fruits Basket* launched and became one of
the best-selling *shōjo* manga ever. While working, Natsuki often
listens to Japanese music and video game soundtracks.

WHAT INFLUENCED YOU TO BECOME A *MANGA-KA?*

Since elementary school, I have loved reading and drawing manga. I slowly came to the realization
that I wanted to make a career out of it. Gradually, it became my dream for the future. It was a hard
road and still is today.

WHAT DOES A DAY IN THE LIFE OF A *MANGA-KA* LOOK LIKE?

When I was drawing *Tsubasa: Those with Wings* and *Fruits Basket*, my days were manga-centered,
meaning I would work on the manga from the moment I woke up. I recklessly took on too much
work and accepted tight deadlines. That led to my physical collapse, forcing me to change how I
approached work.

WHAT SKILLS AND QUALITIES ARE NEEDED TO SUCCEED AS A *MANGA-KA?*

It goes without saying that to start, you must draw. So, I think one needs drawing skills and the
ability to keep drawing.

HOW DID YOUR LIFE CHANGE AFTER *FRUITS BASKET* BECAME A BIG HIT?

Many people have now read my manga and recognize me as someone who draws manga.

WHAT ADVICE WOULD YOU GIVE CHILDREN WHO WANT TO BECOME *MANGA-KA?*

I want to tell them that I want to read the manga that only they can draw. I look forward to the day I
can read it.

MAKE YOUR OWN *YON-KOMA MANGA!*

If you are interested in drawing your own manga, *yon-koma* is the best way to start. The basic principle of *yon-koma* is *Ki-Shō-Ten-Ketsu*.

KI (起):

The first panel starts the story and introduces the place, characters, and situation that will follow.

SHŌ (承):

The story advances from the ki *panel—for example, another character may appear, or a problem may arise.*

TEN (転):

Following the first and second panels, the story takes a turn—something surprising occurs, someone suddenly makes a strong statement, or there is a new disturbance.

KETSU (結):

Because this is a four-panel structure, the story must wrap up in the final panel. The story may finish on an amusing note called ochi *(the punch line).*

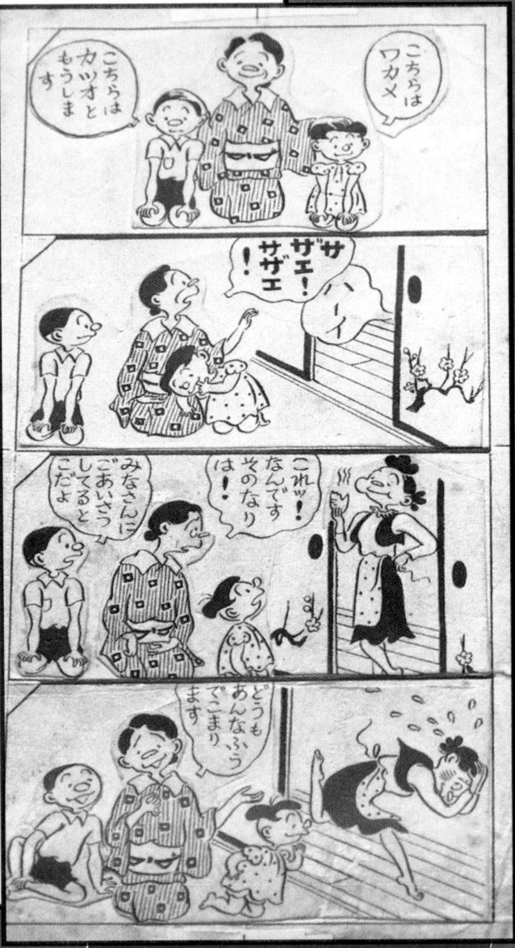
こちらはワカメ
こちらはカツオともうします
サザエ！サザエ！
ハーイ
これッ！なんですそのなりは！
みなさんにごあいさつしてるとこだよ
どうもあんなふうでこまります

An example of a *yon-koma* manga, as well as the first *Sazae-san* manga strip

SO SUGOI!

Many universities offer manga courses, but Kyoto Seika University is Japan's first (and only) university to establish a Faculty of Manga. The faculty consists of *manga-ka* and animators who have created numerous masterpieces, allowing students to learn professional skills directly from the masters. Besides drawing techniques, students study the industry, the history of the works, and how to create hit projects.

EDITOR

Editors are responsible for guiding manga—or any type of book—from the initial idea to the finished product. They are the first readers to work on the story and provide feedback to the *manga-ka*. They work with *manga-ka* to develop the plot and characters to attract new and longtime readers and hold their attention.

Editors should be passionate about what they do and the stories they work on. For a manga to succeed, an editor must believe in it and see its full potential.

INTERVIEW
EDITOR ALEXIS KIRSCH

Alexis Kirsch was born in California and spent his elementary school years in Japan, where he learned Japanese and developed a love of manga. Alexis entered the English manga industry as an editor and translator for TOKYOPOP in 2003 before joining VIZ Media in 2009. After many years as a *Shōnen Jump* editor, Alexis became the editor in chief of English *Shōnen Jump* in 2022.

WHAT WAS YOUR FAVORITE MANGA GROWING UP, AND WHAT IS YOUR CURRENT FAVORITE MANGA THAT YOU WORK ON?

The first manga I really got into was a *Shōnen Jump* series called *Kinnikuman*. This manga series was never released in the United States, but toys based on it called M.U.S.C.L.E. figures were supposedly quite popular here. There was also a sequel series called *Ultimate Muscle* that was released in the 2000s. I collected the entire set of 36 books of this series in the late '80s, and I still own them today. I also became a huge fan of *Dragon Ball* around the same time. I got back into manga in the late '90s, when I realized I could buy the parts of *Dragon Ball* that I hadn't read in the bookshops of Little Tokyo in Los Angeles. I'm currently working on some really fun series like *One Piece* and *Black Clover*. I really enjoy seeing the reactions from the fans with every new chapter.

WHAT MADE YOU INTERESTED IN BECOMING A MANGA EDITOR?

I spent a lot of my childhood in Japan, where I became a huge manga fan. When I returned to the US, I forgot about manga for a few years until I was reintroduced to it in college. Then after college, I looked into ways to make a career out of something that I really enjoyed. I was lucky enough to get an opportunity at TOKYOPOP, where I worked for about five years. I started as a copy editor and translator, then became an editor. I eventually moved on to another manga company, VIZ Media, where I started working on *Shōnen Jump* properties. This was a dream come true, since *Shōnen Jump* had been my favorite manga brand since I was a kid. I would go on to edit series like *Naruto*, *Bleach*, and *One Piece* and would even get to interview some of my favorite creators.

WHAT DOES A DAY IN THE LIFE OF A MANGA EDITOR LOOK LIKE?

Shōnen Jump is a weekly printed magazine in Japan. The challenging aspect to working on it in English is that we release that content simultaneously with Japan in a digital format. This means tight deadlines and repeating the same process or routine every week. We get the files from Japan about a week before we need to go live. The editor will alert the translator and hopefully get a translated script in a few days. The editor reviews that script and sends it to a letterer, who places the English text in the word balloons. The editor then receives a PDF of the chapter, reviews the content, and sends it to a copy editor and an additional editor for further checking. The editor then makes sure all corrections are completed and uploads the file in the final format. There's one additional check that is done before the chapter is signed off on. Each editor works on three to five series and repeats this process multiple times each week. Getting to read comics for a living is very fun, but it is a lot of work.

WHAT ARE SOME OF THE CHALLENGES YOU FACE WHEN INTRODUCING MANGA IN THE US?

This has always been tricky, and we've learned a lot over the years. Some might think that the challenge is when the series is too "Japanese." In fact, back in the old days, companies would flip the art or change all the character names to ones an English speaker would be familiar with. Funnily enough, this aspect doesn't seem to hurt a series at all. Sometimes we even release a series with the title still in Japanese—*Demon Slayer: Kimetsu no Yaiba* is one of our all-time best-selling series.

Many fans seem to like reading a series that feels distinct from what they are used to. When we evaluate a new series, we currently look for one that has a strong story or art and has had some success in Japan or other countries. The only aspect we are really critical of is the genre. Goofy comedy and sports series will sometimes struggle to find an audience here, but there are many exceptions to that as well.

WHAT HAS BEEN YOUR MOST GRATIFYING EXPERIENCE AS A MANGA EDITOR?

Being able to hold a printed book in your hand after months of working on it is always gratifying, but that becomes commonplace after a while. The most gratifying experience for us actually happens outside of the office when we go to conventions and fan events. There's so much passion out there for manga and anime, and it always reinvigorates you when you come in contact with it. These series and characters mean so much to so many people, and just being a part of that is truly special. It's touching when kids ask for my autograph, but I'm just the editor!

TRANSLATOR

To bring manga to non-Japanese-speaking readers, publishers translate the original Japanese script into other languages. This is the responsibility of a translator.

Being an expert in Japanese and another language is essential, but translating text is much more than converting words from one language to another. Translators need to know how dialogue works and fix speech that reads awkwardly. They should also be knowledgeable about two cultures and understand what works in each because nuances in the Japanese language and culture may not be evident to foreign readers.

INTERVIEW
TRANSLATOR MARI MORIMOTO, DVM

Dr. Mari Morimoto was born in Osaka, Japan, but raised in New York City. A freelance translator of manga and Japanese culture content for over 20 years, Mari has translated many best-selling titles such as *Naruto, Dragon Ball, Inuyasha, and Sailor Moon into* English, as well as interpreted for manga and anime creators at conventions.

Mari is a graduate of Cornell University, where zhe obtained both a bachelors degree in anthropology, as well as a doctorate in veterinary medicine. When zhe's not helping animals as a veterinarian, Mari volunteers zir time with veterinary/animal-related, Japanese community, and LGBTQIA+ organizations; traveling; trying new restaurants; and crafting.

WHAT MADE YOU INTERESTED AND HOW DID YOU BECOME A MANGA TRANSLATOR?

To be honest, I never anticipated becoming a manga, or any other sort of, translator. One of my dream careers as a child was to be a *manga-ka* but my drawing skills were inadequate.

I became a manga translator through pure luck and circumstance. While attending college, a professor asked me if I had any interest in manga or anime. I thought it was a trick question, as I had been told by another professor that manga and anime were not academic subjects. It turned out that the professor had a former student who was looking for someone to pick up manga translation work that they couldn't fulfill. That former student put me in touch with VIZ Media, and the rest is history.

WHAT DOES A DAY OF A MANGA TRANSLATOR LOOK LIKE?

It varies quite a bit based on a few factors, such as whether you have a weekly or monthly series that is being released in your region simultaneously with Japan, or a standalone story or series that was published in the past. Either way, a manga translator must keep the schedules and deadlines provided by the editor/publisher.

Many of us have other jobs in addition to manga translation, but when I dedicate part or the entirety of my day to translating, it can involve reading previous volumes, reading ahead, and researching, as well as actually translating dialogue, text, and sound effects. Even though I do most of my research online now, I have printed references and resource materials that I still flip through occasionally.

Depending on the title and publisher, once I have completed and proofread the script, I forward it to either the editor or the letterer. Sometimes I will get questions or requests from the editor for alternate translations of a term or for translation notes. With some series, if the schedules allows it, I even get access to the lettered pages to copyedit and make my own suggestions for changes.

WHAT DO YOU PAY THE MOST ATTENTION TO WHEN TRANSLATING MANGA? WHY IS THAT?

Everything! But if I absolutely had to narrow it down to a few specific items, it would be the "voice" of the series and of the individual characters, the worldview, the genre, and the target audience. I also alert the editor as soon as I skim the chapter or book—and before I start on the script—if there is any content or dialogue that is discriminatory, culturally insensitive, or otherwise inappropriate. Above all, I strive for consistency. This can become quite challenging in a long series and in chapters or volumes that are released infrequently. Personally, I create spreadsheets with different tabs for names of characters, places, attacks, as well as terms, quotes and speech mannerisms, summaries of chapters and volumes, and story arcs. I also have a completely separate spreadsheet just for sound effects and onomatopoeia.

HOW DO YOU HANDLE CULTURAL AND DIALOGUE DIFFERENCES THAT APPEAR IN MANGA SO THAT READERS CAN FOLLOW THE STORY?

Whenever I start a series or standalone project, I always have a discussion with the editor regarding what direction they want to take, so that expectations are clear from the get-go. This is because different publishers, and sometimes editors, handle cultural references differently. For example, some publishers use translation notes at the end of each volume, while others incorporate an explanation within the speech bubble or between panel rows. In addition, some publishers and editors take the position of not translating or incorporating explanations of cultural references at all, because there are fans who prefer to look things up on their own.

Where it can get complicated are references to or differences involving a culture other than that of Japan. An example of this is *The Rose of Versailles*. This manga was particularly challenging because it was written and drawn by a Japanese woman in the early 1970s about the life of Marie Antoinette, based on a 1932 biography by a male Austrian historian. In this case, I prioritized providing an accurate translation, and just added footnotes where the story diverted from actual history.

In terms of dialogue differences, specifically speech mannerisms and dialects, this too varies between editors and publishers, as well as translators. For example, how to represent the Kansai dialect—a dialect of Kyoto, Osaka, and several other prefectures—in English is one of the most hotly debated topics among industry professionals and fans. I am of the school that incorporates "Southern accent"–like speech for the Kansai dialect, and as I am myself Kansai born, I feel justified by my choice.

WHAT HAS BEEN YOUR MOST GRATIFYING EXPERIENCE AS A MANGA TRANSLATOR? WHY?

Many of my most gratifying experiences were related to feeling successful at translating difficult passages or projects—for example, Killer Bee's raps in *Naruto*.

I was also extremely thankful when the publisher Vertical defended my take on a dialect I chose in Osamu Tezuka-sensei's *Ayako* against a negative post. What was interesting about that is that it turns out the "dialect" Tezuka-sensei himself used was not a real dialect, either.

I also enjoy when I am able to use my background in animal health and interest in all things animal related in both my translation and interpreting work. For example, some of the supporting characters in *Cage of Eden* were long-extinct prehistoric animals; it was a lot of fun fact-checking their introductions that were included in every volume.

WHAT ADVICE DO YOU HAVE FOR OUR READERS THAT ARE INTERESTED IN PURSUING MANGA TRANSLATION?

Start learning Japanese right away and keep up with it! In addition to anime, watch live television and films with subtitles. Immerse yourself in the culture, not just in the language. If there is a Japan society or Japanese consulate in your area, try to attend their events, and think about studying abroad at some point. At the same time, do not give up on your other passions and interests, as manga translation is often a side or part-time career. Finally, one thing that now exists that did not when I started out are translation contests, where the reward is a contract with an established publisher.

Good luck!

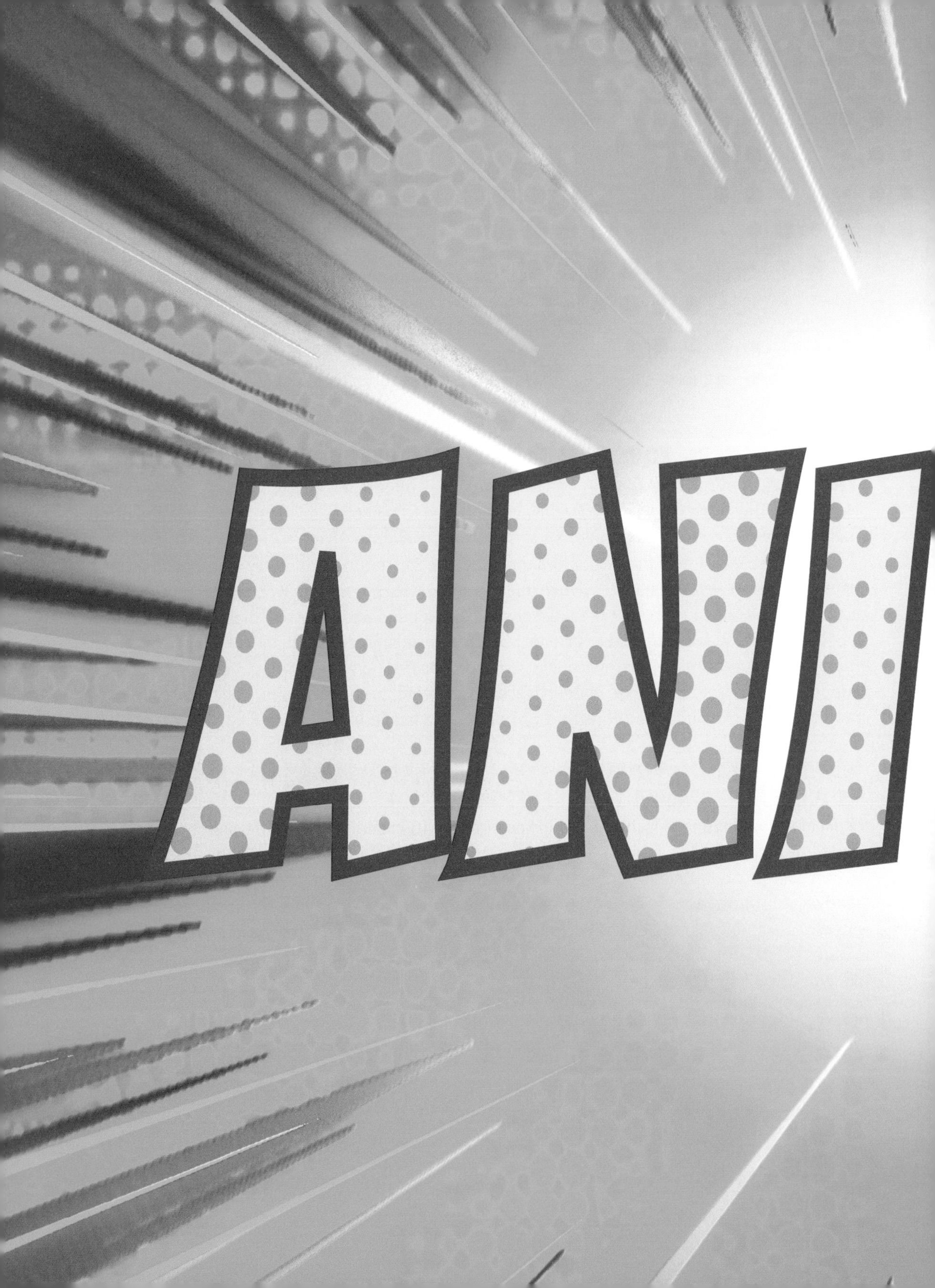
ANI

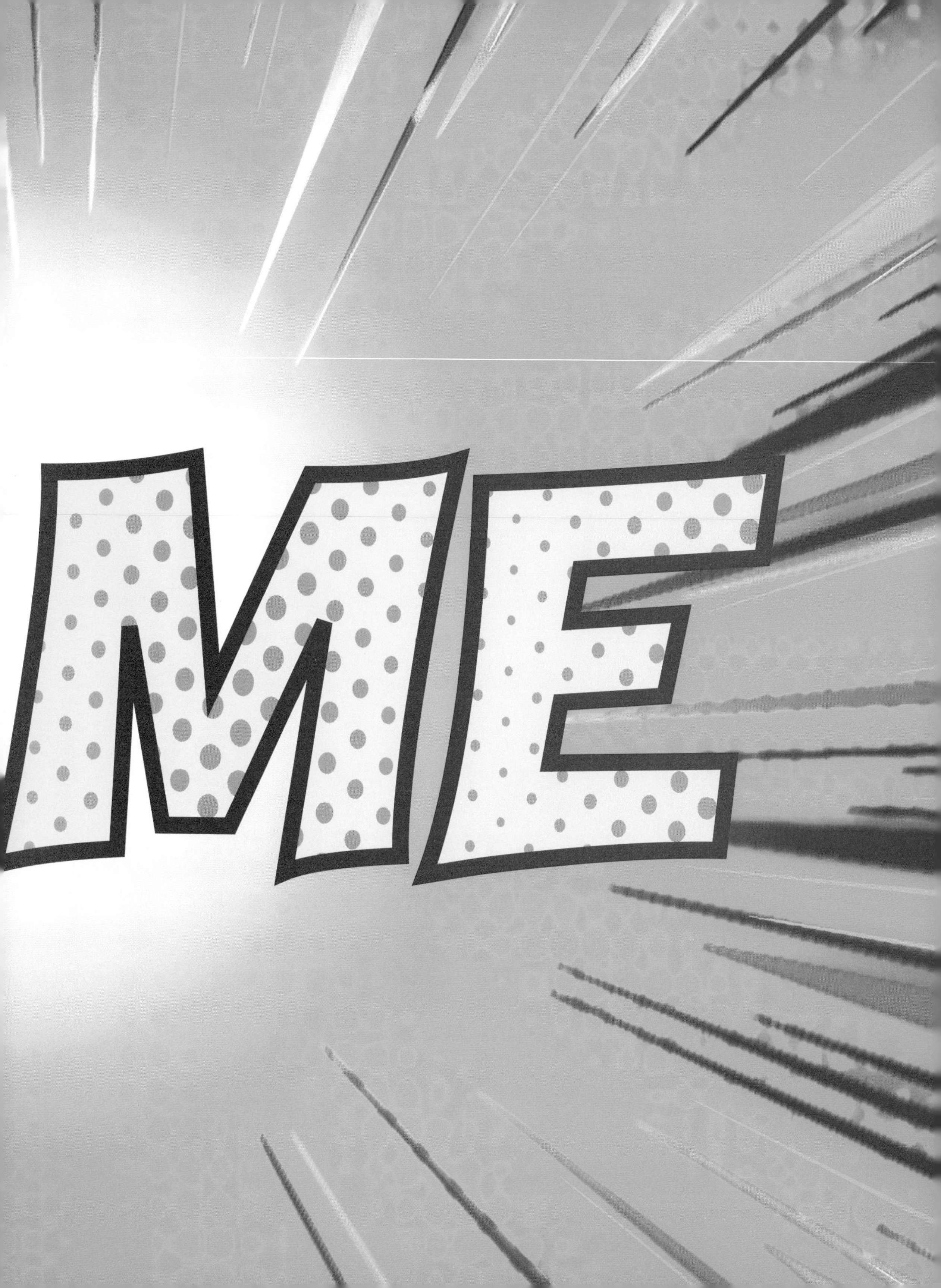
ME

THE DEFINITION OF ANIME

アニメって何？

The term *anime* refers to Japanese animation. Foreign animations, such as *Popeye* and *The Flintstones*, were introduced to Japan around 1960, but the first Japanese TV animation, *Astro Boy* by Osamu Tezuka, did not debut until 1963. Animations broadcast on television were initially called "TV manga"; the word *anime*, short for animation, came into use in the mid-1970s and became a common term in the 1980s. Since the birth of anime, talented creators have led Japanese anime to the pinnacle of animation art. Anime has evolved into one of Japan's leading pop culture genres with worldwide appeal.

Anime became popular outside Japan for several reasons. One reason is that anime appeals to all age groups. Although many anime are created for children—such as *Doraemon* and *Pokémon*—many also attract adult audiences.

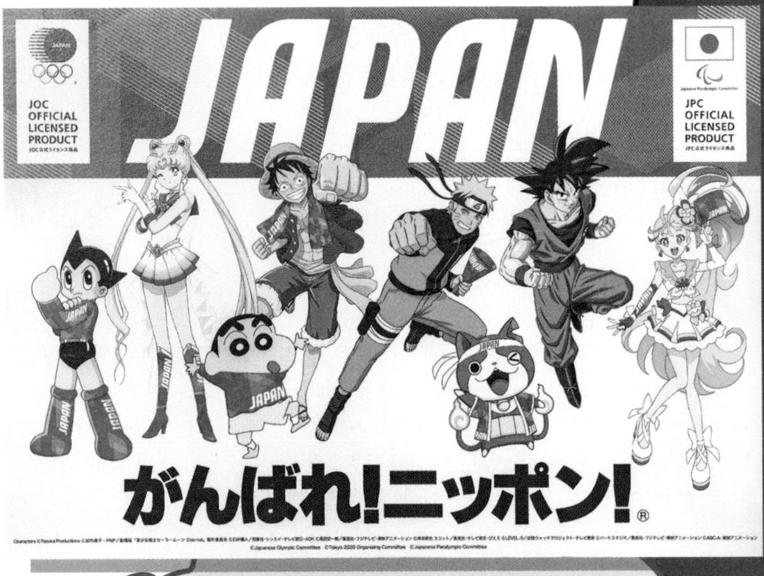

JAPAN
JOC OFFICIAL LICENSED PRODUCT
JPC OFFICIAL LICENSED PRODUCT
がんばれ!ニッポン!

SO SUGOI!

Popular anime characters were selected as official ambassadors for the Tokyo Olympics in 2021. The characters were Sailor Moon, *Dragon Ball*'s Son Goku, *Astro Boy*'s Astro, *One Piece*'s Luffy, Crayon Shinchan, Naruto, *Yo-kai Watch*'s Jibanyan, and Pretty Cure.

Anime comprises a wide variety of genres, including romance, action, fantasy, comedy, and science fiction. Interestingly, the hero in anime doesn't always win; sometimes the main character loses a battle or even dies. Anime stories are often unpredictable and complex—yet another reason they inspire a huge and devoted international following.

Although anime are produced on limited budgets, they are generally high-quality products in terms of illustrations and stories. Overseas animation studios tend to invest heavily in a large staff and computer graphics, while production costs for Japanese films are modest—for example, Disney's *Tangled* cost $260 million to make, while Studio Ghibli's *Spirited Away* only cost $19 million. Japanese anime creators must produce high-quality products at a relatively low production cost. The quality of these artists' work cannot be replicated by computers, no matter how large the budget. This is one more reason fans are so enamored by Japanese anime.

In 2020, Japan produced 278 anime television shows and 66 anime movies. Impressive, isn't it? Many anime are based on manga, and the two art forms are strongly connected. As anime have exploded in popularity worldwide, people have become more interested in Japan, along with the Japanese language and culture.

Let's get started by learning about the history of anime and how it earned its reputation and global popularity!

THE BEGINNINGS OF JAPANESE ANIMATION

アニメのはじまり

In 1896, the first moving picture was imported from overseas and released in Japan. Because of this, interest in movies grew, and theaters featured numerous foreign animated films, such as 1912's *The Nipper's Transformations* from France and *Colonel Heeza Liar* from the United States in 1913. Japanese anime was born due to the influence of these imported animated films.

Japanese filmmakers were not about to overlook the popularity of foreign animation. In 1917, three separate works were released by three founders of Japanese animation: Hekoten Shimokawa, Seitarō Kitayama, and Jun'ichi Kōuchi.

The oldest Japanese animated film we can view today is Jun'ichi Kōuchi's *The Dull Sword* (*Namakura Gatana*), originally released in June 1917. The story is comical and straightforward: A samurai gets tricked into buying a sword and uses it to attack passersby, but the blade can't cut anyone. The sword is bent out of shape, and the poor samurai gets beaten up. In 2008, only *The Dull Sword*'s second half was available, having been discovered at an antique market in Osaka. Luckily, the first half was found in 2014, allowing technicians to restore a near-complete version of the film.

The characters in *The Dull Sword* were made from paper cutouts, which allowed them to move around freely. The motion of the eyes, mouths, wrinkles, and other details is smooth from frame to frame. Stars appear when a character gets hit, and the bent sword spins around when the hero is defeated. These and other expressive attributes could only be achieved through animation techniques. The characters also had large heads and eyes, like in current anime.

Up until the start of World War II, American animation was popular in Japan, but the situation changed once

SO SUGOI!

In addition to Manga Day, Japan also has an Anime Day, on October 22! Anime Day was established in 2017 to commemorate the release of Japan's first color feature-length animated film, *The White Snake Enchantress*, on October 22, 1958. Anime Day's purpose is to foster the appeal of Japanese anime throughout the world.

war broke out and American films were banned. In 1943, Kenzō Masaoka, known as the "Father of Japanese Animation," released the black-and-white animated film *The Spider and the Tulip* (*Kumo to Tulip*). This musical animation in which ladybugs and spiders sing established the hand-drawn animation style that uses transparent celluloid sheets (cels). Cels were a precious commodity at the time, so they were washed and reused.

Movie stills from *The Dull Sword*, courtesy of the National Film Archive of Japan

In 1945, just before the war's end, materials were in extremely short supply, including those needed for film production. Despite this, the Japanese Navy managed to release *Momotaro: Sacred Sailors* (*Momotarō: Umi no Shinpei*), and it was the first feature-length Japanese animation film shown in cinemas. The teenage Osamu Tezuka was moved to tears watching the movie in a cinema that had survived the wartime devastation. He wondered how Japan came to produce such brilliant work. This experience inspired him to become an anime creator.

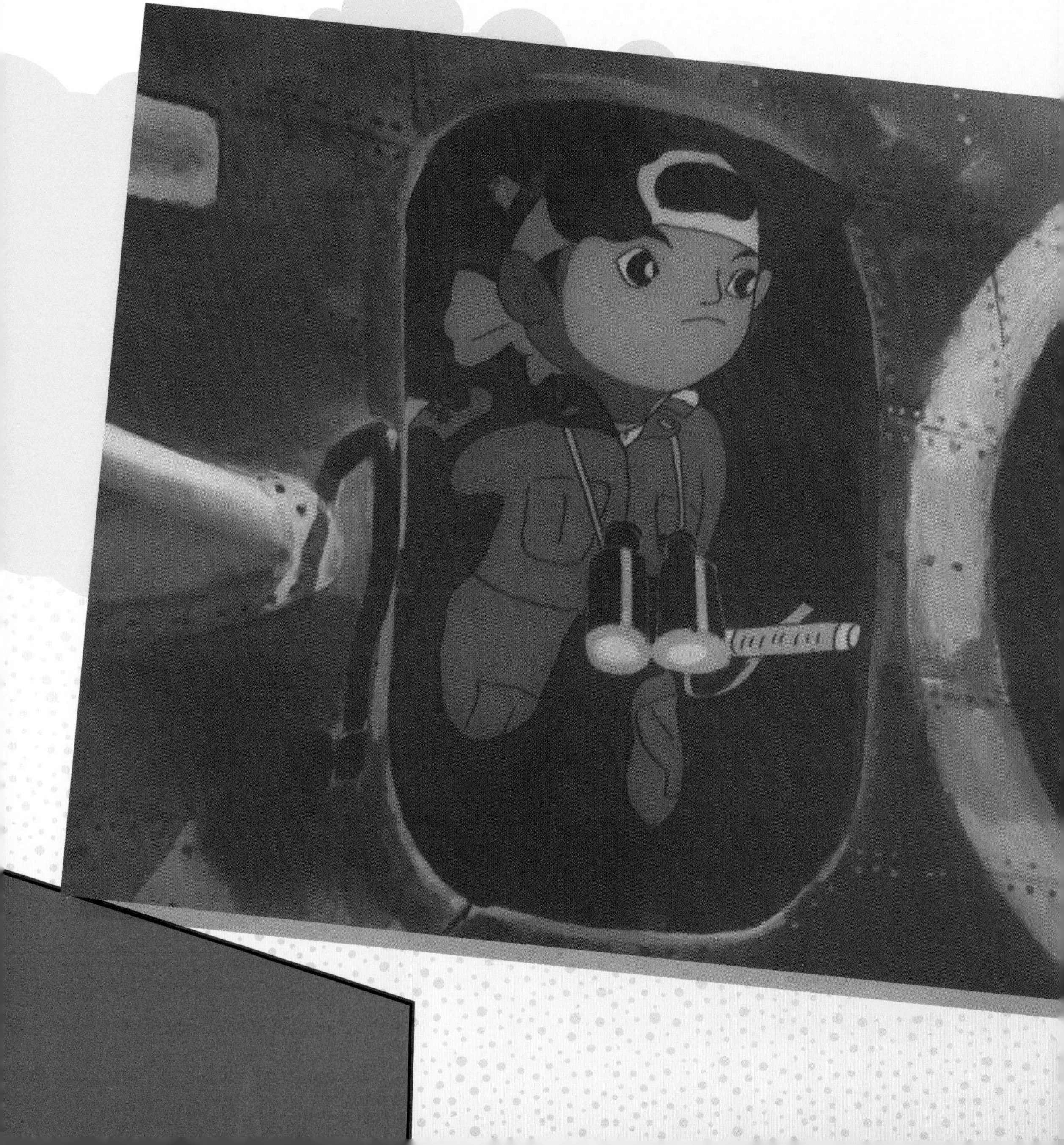

Toei Doga Studio (now Toei Animation) was founded in 1956. The studio was greatly influenced by the Disney animated film *Snow White* (1937) and set its sights on becoming the "Disney of the East." In 1958, Toei released Japan's first all-color, feature-length animated theatrical film, *The White Snake Enchantress* (*Hakujaden*). The success of *The White Snake Enchantress* convinced Toei to produce a theatrical animated feature every year. The Japanese animation industry was off and running!

Left: Movie still from *Momotaro: Sacret Sailors*, courtesy of Shochiku Co., Ltd.
© 1945/2016 Shochiku Co., Ltd.

Above: Movie still from *The Spider and the Tulip*, courtesy of Shochiku Co., Ltd.
© 1943/2012 Shochiku Co., Ltd.

OSAMU TEZUKA'S INFLUENCE ON ANIME

手塚治虫の影響

Although Toei Doga Studio created animated films to entertain children, one film a year was not enough. This is where weekly TV animation came into the picture. Manga had already entered the era of weekly publication, so weekly animated series were sure to follow.

Osamu Tezuka's *Astro Boy* premiered on Japanese television on January 1, 1963, and ran for four years. It marked the transition from foreign animation to homegrown anime culture. Initially, Disney's work inspired Tezuka to pursue animation, but when the time came to produce his own animated movie, due to budgetary constraints he did not follow in Disney's footsteps. A Disney-type animated film requires a massive budget and production staff. Despite Tezuka's success as a *manga-ka*, he did not have the resources to create an anime film on his own.

Tezuka saw that an opportunity to air an animated series came with television rather than movies. Before *Astro Boy*, Japanese television was broadcasting five- to ten-minute foreign-made TV cartoons like *Popeye*. These cartoons were too brief to develop an authentic story, so their comedic effects relied on gags and comic movements. Tezuka had no interest in that; he believed like serialized manga, a weekly series could be story-driven.

Right and across: Astro Boy anime stills courtesy of Tezuka Productions

© Tezuka Productions

Tezuka's first animation was a half-hour episode broadcast every Tuesday from 6:15 to 6:45 p.m. He decided to adapt his manga *Astro Boy* into an animated TV series. Tezuka's series was the first of its kind and laid the groundwork for the emergence of a new world of Japanese animated programs. This fulfilled a long-held dream Tezuka had to create an animation! Besides his unshakable position as a leading *manga-ka*, he was now also Japan's top animator.

In addition to accomplishing the first animated TV series, Tezuka and his staff also developed a cost-cutting method to minimize the number of drawings required to produce a weekly 30-minute program. They recycled celluloid sheets (cels) from scene to scene as much as possible, keeping the images simple. They also tried to compress story development and used music, sound effects, and dialogue to generate the sensation of movement. By limiting movements and special effects, they reduced the number of cels required to produce an anime. With these innovations, Tezuka overcame the staffing and production cost constraints. These methods became known as Japanese-style "limited animation" and made mass production viable.

Tezuka also made up for the lack of a budget (he still had a budget, it just wasn't a big budget) by earning licensing income from character merchandise. He granted companies the right to market *Astro Boy* characters in advertisements and products. He also generously devoted some of his manga publishing profits to foster new animation production.

It was not an easy road, but these innovations and methods arose from the desire to entertain viewers. As a result, Japanese animation evolved into *anime*, with its own unique characteristics, unrivaled anywhere else in the world.

After *Astro Boy*, many animated series were produced, and an era of fierce competition ensued. In the fall of 1963, *8 Man*, *Wolf Boy Ken*, and *Tetsujin 28*, Japan's first giant robot anime, were broadcast, and all captured the hearts of children. In 1965, 14 new anime series were released. Together with the ongoing broadcasts, up to 20 titles were being aired—a milestone in the Japanese anime industry! In the same year, Japan's first full-color TV series, *Jungle Emperor*—another creation of Osamu Tezuka—was released, as well as *Little Ghost Q-Taro* (*Obake no Kyū-Tarō*), Japan's first comedy anime, which also began the format of airing two 15-minute shows per episode.

The new anime industry was booming!

THE HISTORY OF ROBOT ANIME
ロボットアニメの歴史

1n 1963, *Astro Boy* was the first TV anime, followed by *Tetsujin 28* that same year. These two robot anime launched the era of profitable TV anime. *Astro Boy* was a humanoid robot with a humanlike will, while *Tetsujin 28* was a giant robot controlled by remote control. In the 1970s, the *manga-ka* Go Nagai (1945–) brought two revolutionary ideas to robot anime.

His first innovation, in *Mazinger Z*, introduced a gigantic robot that could be piloted. The second was the "combining robot," in which multiple fighter machines, or mecha (pronounced *meh-kuh*), combine into a single giant machine. This appeared in Nagai's memorable *Getter Robo*, in which three combat Getter Machines formed into one giant robot.

MAZINGER Z
(*Majingā Zetto*, 1972)

To confront Dr. Hell, who is plotting to take over the world, Dr. Kabuto makes the giant robot Mazinger Z. His grandson Kōji boards the robot as its pilot, and together they fight Dr. Hell and his army of mechanical beasts. This is the first super-giant robot anime in the history of TV anime.

GETTER ROBO
(*Gettā Robo*, 1974)

A combining robot named Getter Robo fights to protect humanity from invasion by the Dinosaur Empire. Three high school students with a strong sense of justice act as pilots, and three airplane-like vehicles called Getter Machines combine to transform into three types of robots: one that operates in the air, one on the ground, and one under the sea.

Japanese anime evolved in a unique direction in the 1970s; the story lines became more elaborate, and the illustrations more detailed and realistic. The emphasis on storytelling led to the creation of new settings and perspectives on life. For example, *Space Battleship Yamato*, which aired in 1974, followed a dramatic and mythological story line in which Earth was on the verge of extinction due to an invasion from outer space. This anime overwhelmingly attracted a young adult audience and helped dismiss the idea that anime was only for children.

Mobile Suit Gundam, a robot anime created for middle and high school students, grew in popularity and attracted adults as well. Before *Gundam*, robots were often depicted as mysterious figures with immense powers. However, *Gundam* introduced a new concept: that robots could be mass produced by humans to fight wars. In *Gundam*, good and evil and friend and foe became blurred, which was considered innovative at the time.

MOBILE SUIT GUNDAM
(*Kidō Senshi Gandamu*, 1979)

A half century after humans began to abandon Earth due to overpopulation, a boy named Amuro Ray accidentally boards the Earth Federation's new mobile suit, Gundam, and becomes its pilot during a surprise attack by the Zeon forces.

The success of *Mobile Suit Gundam* and *Space Battleship Yamato* demonstrated that anime targeting young adults could be profitable as long as they used complex stories, artwork, and characters that kept viewers engaged.

Following the *Gundam* blockbuster of the 1980s, a series of *Gundam* sequels appeared in the 1990s. While robot anime for younger audiences were released one after another, many robot anime with more realistic settings were also produced. As the generation that watched robot anime in the '70s and '80s grew up, they appreciated this more lifelike angle and enjoyed imagining these giant robots inhabiting the real world one day.

Mobile Suit Gundam © SOTSU-SUNRISE

In the 21st century, many robot anime have shifted their focus from battle scenes to the emotional aspects of their human characters. These characters face personal issues, and the stories dig deeper into those issues as the plot advances. Also at this time, some studios remade earlier iconic Japanese anime like *Astro Boy*, *Tetsujin 28*, and *Mazinger Z*.

HERE COME THE MAGICAL GIRLS
魔法少女の登場

Most people who follow anime have heard about magical girls. Magical girls (*mahō shōjo* or *majokko*) are female characters who appear in works set in the modern world and use superhuman magic or other mysterious powers. It's such a popular genre among young girls that several masterpieces sparked social phenomena during their releases. As times changed, magical girl stories diversified to capture the interest of male fans as well.

The first magical girl anime was *Sally the Witch* (*Mahōtsukai Sarī*), released in 1966. It was the story of a girl from a magical land who set out to help people in the human world. In the early days of the magical girl genre, the standard story line involved a girl using supernatural powers to solve people's problems. Later, a new type of anime appeared in which ordinary human girls accidentally obtained magical powers, like the protagonist of *The Secrets of Akko-chan* (*Himitsu no Akko-chan*, 1969), who acquired a magical mirror that allowed her to transform into other beings. Compared to *Sally*, the girls featured in *Akko-chan* resembled everyday kids.

In the 1970s, the anime *Majokko Megu-chan* struck a chord with viewers. The story concerned two female protagonists, Megu and Non, both candidates to become the next queen of the magical worlds. They fought together in battles and, on occasion, tormented each other—a groundbreaking plotline at the time. In previous anime, girls rarely formed deep friendships like these two. However, by the 1970s, women were assuming a more prominent role in society, and girls sought out heroines who took control of their lives and enjoyed the camaraderie of other heroines rather than spending all their time pursuing boyfriends.

Japan experienced an idol boom in the 1980s, and girls aspired to dress and act like teenage pop singers, like the ones found in *Magical Princess Minky Momo* and *Creamy Mami, the Magic Angel*. These *majokko* characters had something in common: they used magic to transform into their adult selves. Both *Minky Momo* and *Creamy Mami* incorporated elements of working women, idols, and the show business world that girls dreamed of being a part of. In doing so, they expanded their target audiences, winning the support not only of children but also of young men.

MAGICAL PRINCESS MINKY MOMO

(Mahō no Purinsesu Minkī Momo, 1982)

Momo, a 12-year-old girl from Dreamland, uses her magical powers to transform into a young adult and solve problems children cannot. By doing so, Momo encourages people on Earth to pursue their dreams and hopes.

CREAMY MAMI, THE MAGIC ANGEL

(Mahō no Tenshi Kurīmī Mami, 1983)

Ten-year-old Yū gains magical powers for a limited period of one year. When she transforms into an older version of herself, she accidentally winds up on TV and debuts as an idol called Creamy Mami. Creamy Mami established an unprecedented idol-like character by immersing itself in the show business world.

There were significant changes to the magical girl genre during the 1990s. Up until that time, magical girl plots revolved mainly around magical phenomena in everyday life. *Sailor Moon* borrowed elements from *shōnen* manga—friendship and conflict between the protagonists—and from hero anime—collaborating to defeat enemies.

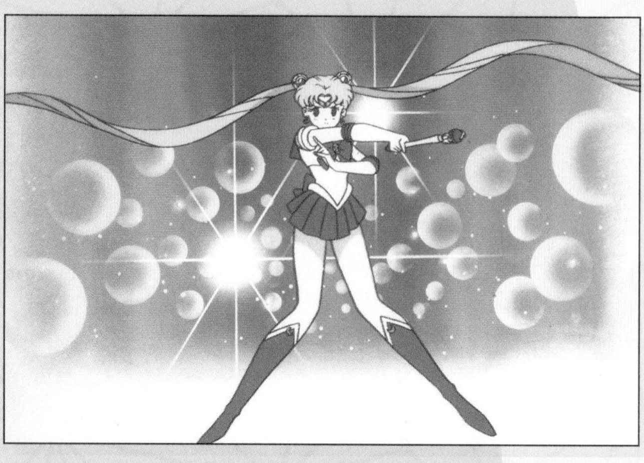

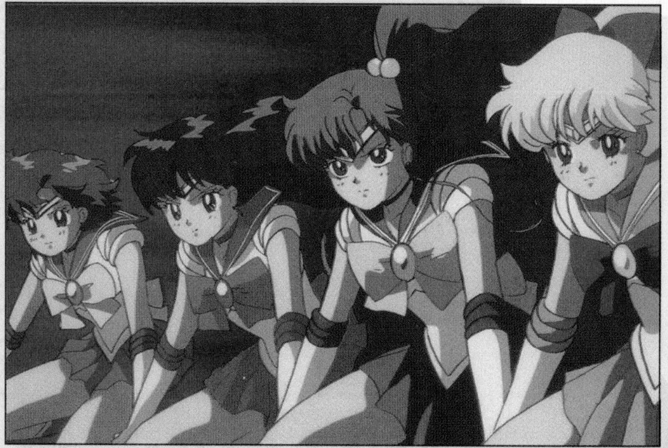

Sailor Moon, based on a popular manga series created by Naoko Takeuchi, aired in 1992, a time when society encouraged women to enter the workforce. Women's perceptions of happiness were evolving, and the anime reflected this. Their dreams were no longer confined to old stereotypes, such as "life's primary goal is marrying the right man." With the success of *Sailor Moon*, protagonists became battling heroines, prompting the release of several fighting magical girl anime.

The heroines of this era mostly used magic to defeat their opponents without actually fighting them physically. This plotline carried over until the *Pretty Cure* series in the 2000s. *Pretty Cure* started the trend of depicting girls participating in intense battles where they fought with their fists without the help of male heroes.

In 2011, another magical girl anime premiered and caused a shake-up. *Puella Magi Madoka Magica* follows junior high school student Madoka and a group of girls with magical powers in their battles against witches. Even though this anime was a fantasy that maintained traditional fairy-tale designs and costumes, it explored serious issues and had shocking developments, like the deaths of key characters. By greatly expanding the boundaries of magical girl plots, *Puella Magi Madoka Magica* astonished anime fans in Japan and worldwide.

At a glance, the history of magical girl anime shows how society has progressed over time, particularly regarding women's roles. This genre reflects the changing aspirations and expectations of their young female viewers!

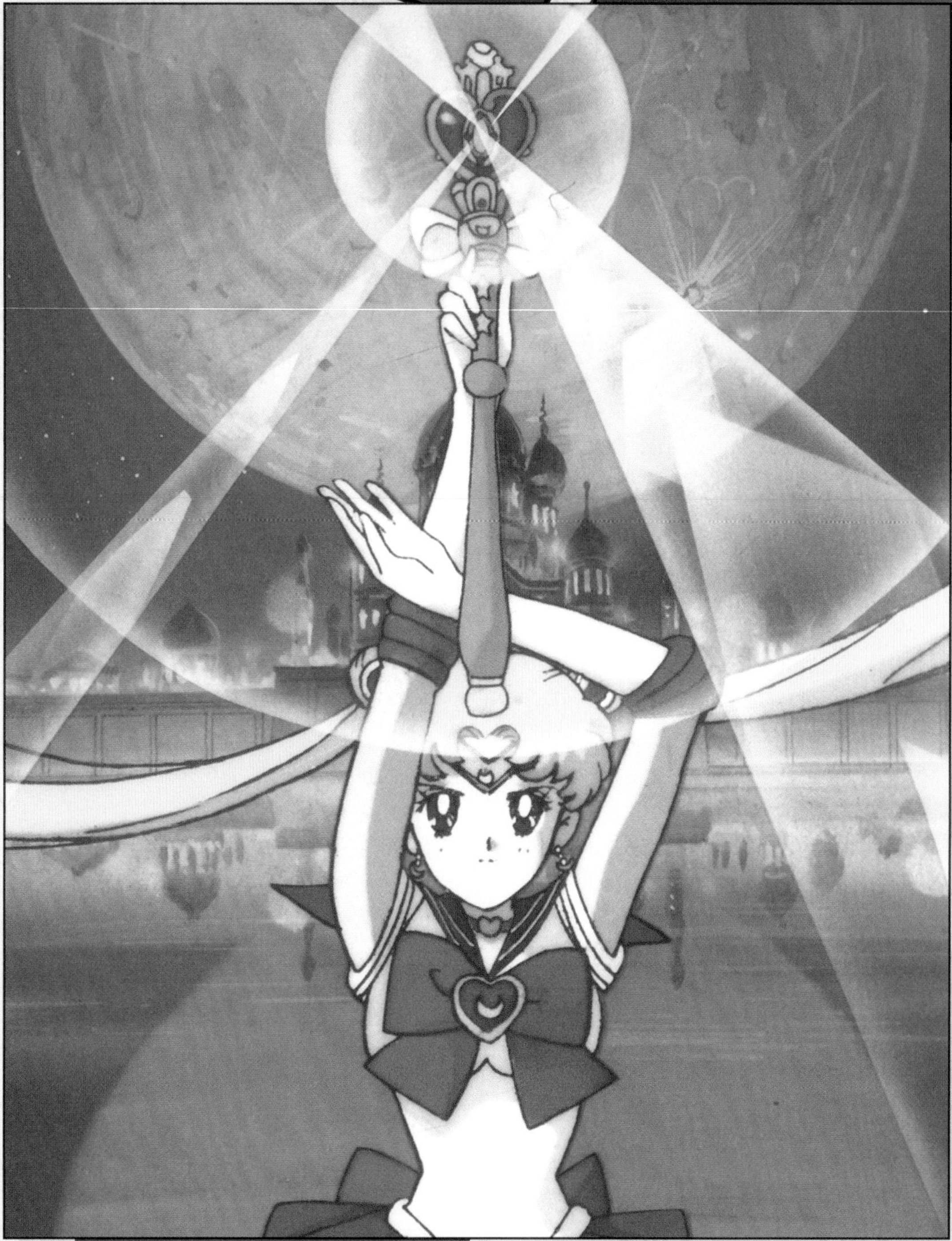

Stills from *Sailor Moon R : The Movie*

ANIME FILMS

アニメ映画

In the 1970s, there was a surge in anime films, but many were reedited versions of TV anime shows. Videocassette recorders were not widespread then, so fans went to theaters to rewatch their favorite TV anime scenes.

In the 1980s and 1990s, new anime films began rolling out. One of them, *AKIRA* (1988), attracted the attention of young American adults for its realism and near-future setting. Until then, people in the United States and around the world had equated animation with family entertainment, as represented by Disney. However, adults could also enjoy *AKIRA* since it was made with a mature audience in mind. At the time, Japan was world-renowned for the miniaturization of electronic devices used in computers and was considered a high-tech country. People saw anime as a natural extension of that.

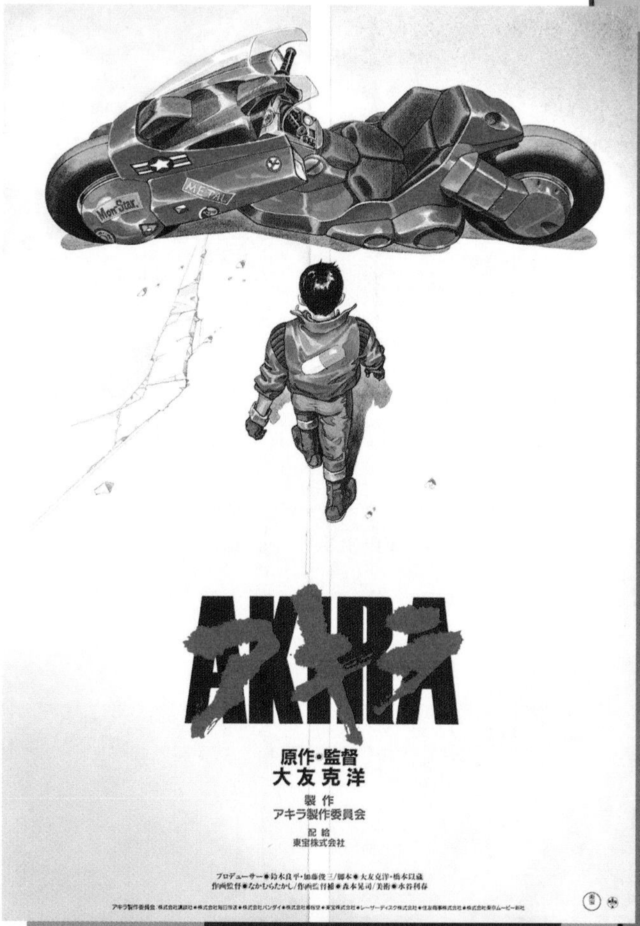
AKIRA
アキラ
原作・監督
大友克洋
製作
アキラ製作委員会
配給
東宝株式会社
Japanese movie poster for *AKIRA*

Despite the popularity of *AKIRA*, most anime films continued to target young audiences, especially those by Hayao Miyazaki of Studio Ghibli, who directed classics like *Nausicaä of the Valley of the Wind* (1984), *Castle in the Sky* (1986), and *My Neighbor Totoro* (1988).

In addition to Studio Ghibli's works, anime films from other studios such as *Doraemon*, *Dragon Ball*, and *Detective Conan* ranked among the top-grossing Japanese films every year.

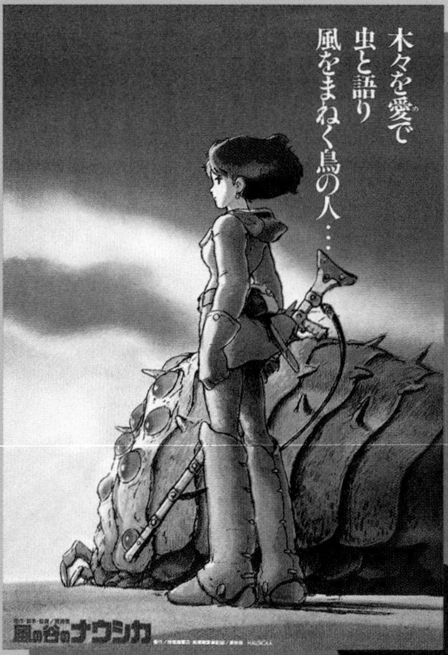
木々を愛で
虫と語り
風をまねく鳥の人…
風の谷のナウシカ

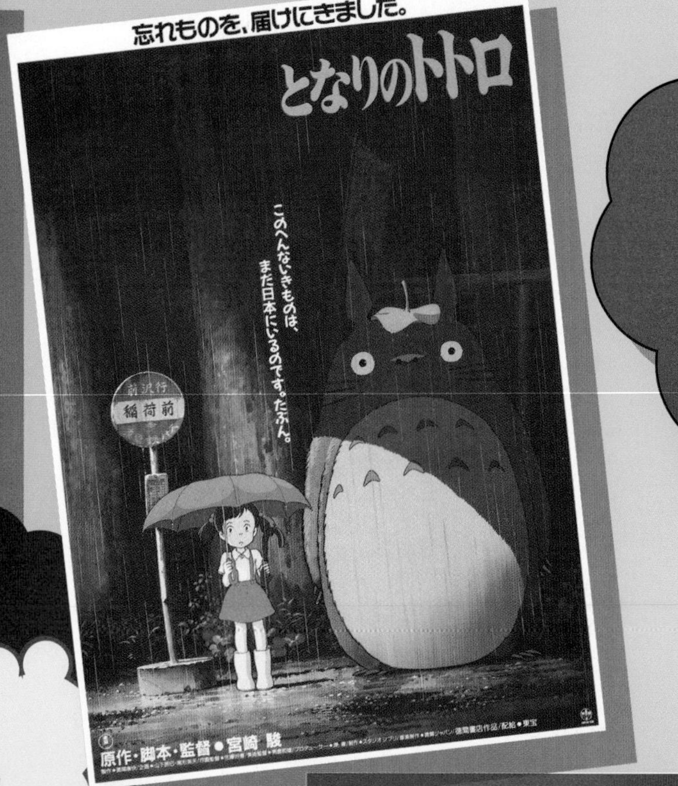
忘れものを、届けにきました。
となりのトトロ
このへんないきものは、まだ日本にいるのです。たぶん。
稲荷前
原作・脚本・監督●宮崎 駿

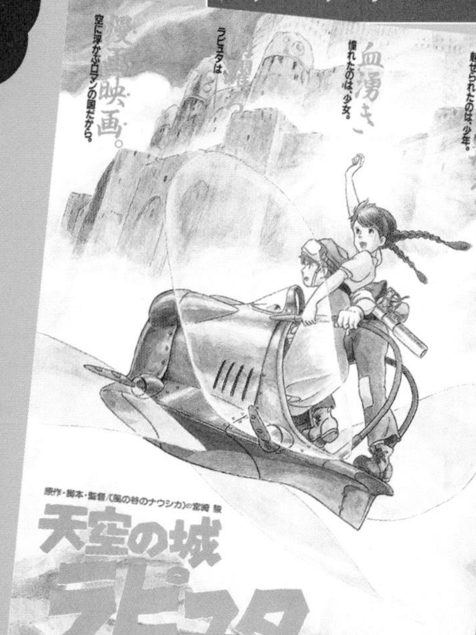
天空の城
ラピュタ

Japanese movie posters for *Nausicaä of the Valley of the Wind*, *Castle in the Sky*, and *My Neighbor Totoro*

SO SUGOI!

The 2020 release of *Demon Slayer: Kimetsu no Yaiba–The Movie: Mugen Train* racked up a whopping $359.7 million in Japan, making it the top-grossing film in Japanese cinematic history! Five other anime films are among Japan's ten most profitable films as of 2022, including *Spirited Away*, *Your Name.*, *Princess Mononoke*, *Howl's Moving Castle*, and *One Piece Film: Red*.

An increasing number of anime films are being released in the United States and raking in high box-office revenues. Here are the five top-grossing anime films in the United States as of 2022. How many of these hit anime films have you seen?

1: *Pokémon: The First Movie*
2: *Demon Slayer: Kimetsu no Yaiba–The Movie: Mugen Train*
3: *Pokémon: The Movie 2000*
4: *Jujutsu Kaisen 0: The Movie*
5: *Dragon Ball Super: Broly*

POKÉMON!

In 1998, *Pokémon: The First Movie* was released in Japanese cinemas and became an instant box-office hit—Japan's highest-grossing anime film that year. This success was replicated in the United States, too, as its 1999 box office revenue was over $85 million, making it the highest-grossing anime film there to date!

POKÉMON: THE FIRST MOVIE

(1998)

This film stands out from the Pokémon animated show due to its serious themes. Mewtwo, a key character in the film, leads a group of cloned Pokémon in a fight against the original Pokémon and a revolt against humans. The film appeared to question the ethics of cloning—a hot topic in the news at the time.

©2018 Pokémon. ©1997, 1998 Nintendo, Creatures, GAME FREAK, TV Tokyo, ShoPro, JR Kikaku. ©PIKACHU PROJECT '98. TM, ®, and character names are trademarks of Nintendo.

ANIME MOVIE DIRECTORS

HAYAO MIYAZAKI
(1941–)

Hayao Miyazaki is one of Japan's leading anime film directors. He has created numerous films at Studio Ghibli, including *Princess Mononoke* and *Spirited Away*. One of the distinguishing features of his early work was his desire to create anime from a child's perspective. Yet, his works are among the world's finest animated films and are beloved by children and adults alike for their beauty and exquisite details.

After graduating from college, Miyazaki began working for Toei Doga, producing the TV anime series *Future Boy Conan* (*Mirai Shōnen Konan*, 1978), and then directing his first film, *Lupin III: The Castle of Cagliostro* (*Rupan Sansei: Kariosutoro no Shiro*), in 1979, which was highly acclaimed. In 1984, he directed the film *Nausicaä of the Valley of the Wind* (*Kaze no Tani no Nausicaä*) based on his own manga. The following year, Miyazaki joined in the founding of Studio Ghibli, which has produced numerous masterpieces. In 1997, the Ghibli production *Princess Mononoke* was released and became a huge box office hit, breaking all records at the time. *Spirited Away*, released in 2001, was also a blockbuster that won an Academy Award for Best Animated Feature in the United States.

Miyazaki is knowledgeable about military history and weaponry, and although many of his works have war as a theme, he is strongly opposed to it— his works frequently highlight the foolishness and misery of war.

In 2022, Ghibli Park, a theme park based on the world of Studio Ghibli, opened in Aichi Prefecture, Japan. It is a dreamlike space where visitors experience the world of Ghibli films while strolling along forest paths!

KIKI'S DELIVERY SERVICE

(*Majo no Takkyūbin*, 1989)

The story follows Kiki, a 13-year-old girl who leaves her parents and struggles to become a full-fledged witch in her new hometown. Her magic is limited to flying on a broomstick and talking to her black cat, Gigi. Despite setbacks, Kiki matures through her encounters with various people in her new living environment.

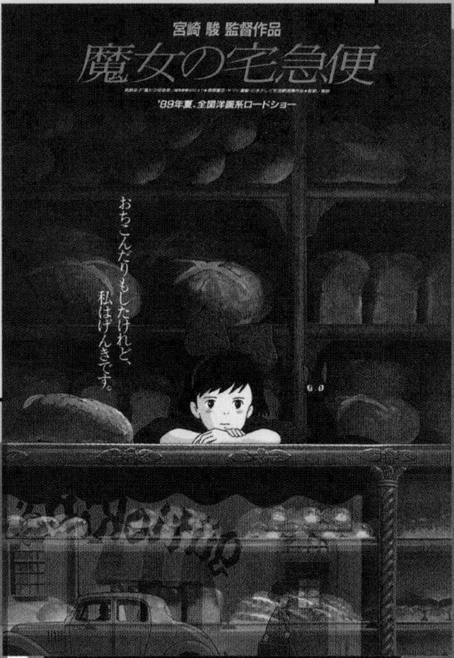
宮崎 駿 監督作品
魔女の宅急便
'89年夏、全国洋画系ロードショー
おちこんだりもしたけれど、私はげんきです。

Japanese movie poster for *Kiki's Delivery Service*

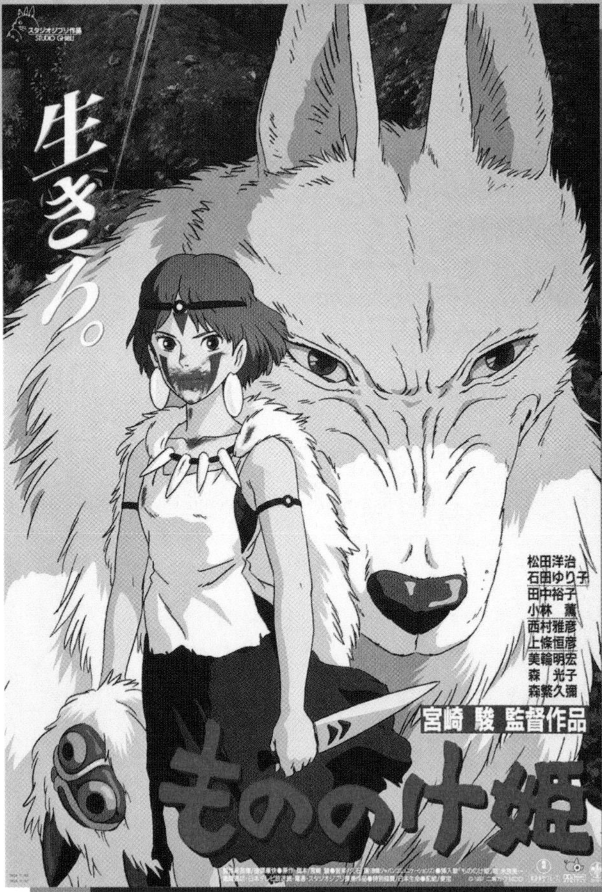
スタジオジブリ作品
STUDIO GHIBLI
生きろ。
松田洋治
石田ゆり子
田中裕子
小林 薫
西村雅彦
上條恒彦
美輪明宏
森 光子
森繁久彌
宮崎 駿 監督作品
もののけ姫

Japanese movie poster for *Princess Mononoke*

PRINCESS MONONOKE

(*Mononoke-hime*, 1997)

In ancient Japan, the people of Irontown are destroying the forest to feed their economy, but they face problems related to discrimination and power struggles. As the film progresses, they search for ways to coexist with nature and build a better future world. The anime's in-depth exploration of themes such as life and death and humanity's relationship to nature is part of its attraction.

スタジオジブリ作品
STUDIO GHIBLI

生あります

トンネルのむこうは、
不思議の町でした。

柊　瑠美
入野自由
夏木マリ
内藤剛志
沢口靖子
菅原文太

宮崎　駿　監督作品

千と千尋の神隠し

製作総指揮　徳間康快●原作・脚本・監督　宮崎　駿●音楽　久石　譲●作画監督　安藤雅司●美術監督　武重洋二●プロデューサー　鈴木敏夫●製作　スタジオジブリ
徳間書店・スタジオジブリ・日本テレビ・電通・ディズニー・東北新社・三菱商事　提供作品　　特別協賛　ネスレ ジャパン グループ　　配給　東宝

© 2001 二馬力・TGNDDTM

Japanese movie poster
for *Spirited Away*

SPIRITED AWAY

(*Sen to Chihiro
no Kamikakushi*,
2001)

*This is a fantasy
film about the
coming-of-age
of a ten-year-old girl. While heading to a new house with her parents, she wanders into a
mysterious town. Her parents are turned into pigs, and a mysterious boy rescues her. This
anime was a catalyst, spreading the word about the marvels of Japanese anime technology.*

HIDEAKI ANNO (1960-)

In 1995, Anno created the TV anime *Neon Genesis Evangelion*, which became a social phenomenon. Having participated in *Nausicaä of the Valley of the Wind*, he looked up to Hayao Miyazaki as his creative mentor. He also wanted to participate in Miyazaki's *The Wind Rises* (*Kaze Tachinu*, 2013) as an animator but was chosen to voice the main character Jirō instead.

Anno has also worked on live-action films such as *Shin Godzilla* (general director, 2016) and *Shin Ultraman* (screenwriter, 2022), both resurrections of famous Japanese movies. His latest live-action film, *Shin Kamen Rider* (director), was released in 2023.

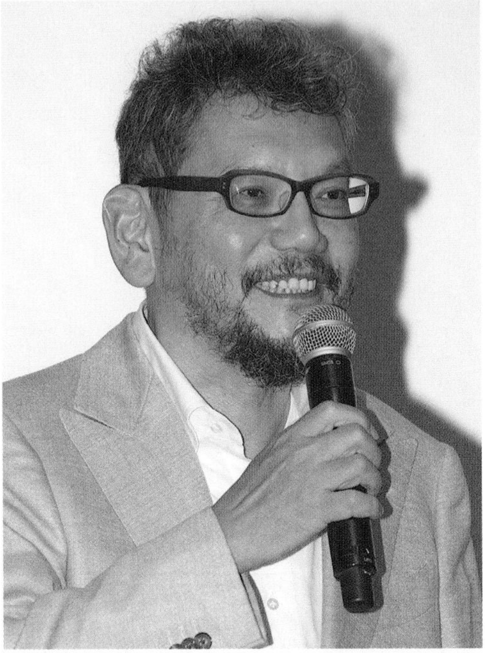

MAMORU HOSODA (1967-)

Hosoda directed anime films such as *Digimon Adventure* and *One Piece* before releasing *The Girl Who Leapt through Time* in 2006, which won several movie awards in Japan and abroad and brought the director worldwide fame. After a string of successes, Hosoda's 2018 *Mirai* was nominated for Best Animated Feature at the 91st Academy Awards in the United States. His films are characterized by their portrayal of relationships and situations with which anyone can relate: the mother-child relationship in *Wolf Children* (2012), the master and disciple in *The Boy and the Beast* (2015), and the struggles of a four-year-old boy in *Mirai* (2018).

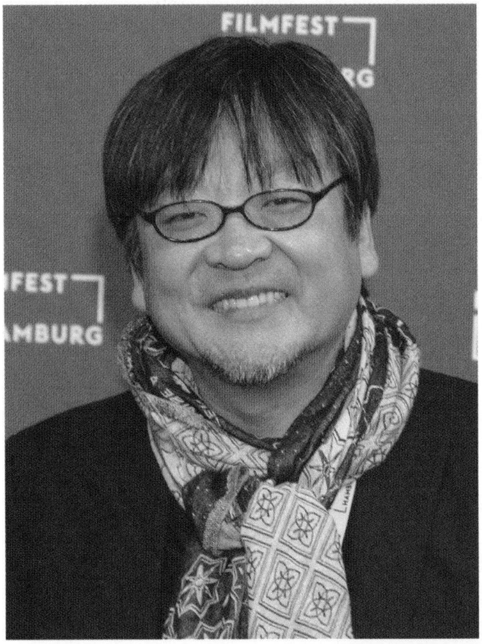
FILMFEST
RG
FEST
MBURG

THE GIRL WHO LEAPT THROUGH TIME
(Toki o Kakeru Shōjo, 2006)

Makoto, a sophomore in high school, has not found what she wants to do nor decided on a career path. One day, the brakes on her bicycle fail, and she is thrown onto a railroad crossing as a train arrives. At that very moment, she finds she is able to leap back in time. What ensues changes her ordinary life drastically.

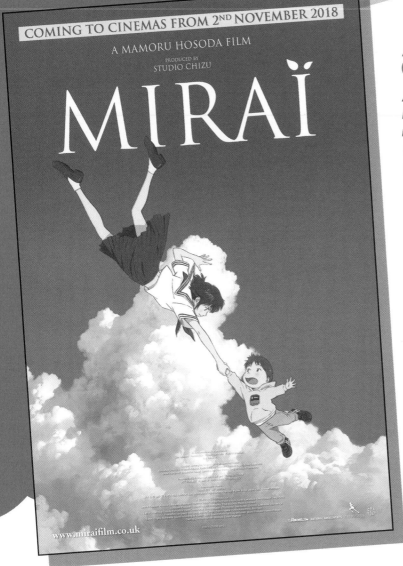

COMING TO CINEMAS FROM 2ND NOVEMBER 2018

A MAMORU HOSODA FILM

PRODUCED BY
STUDIO CHIZU

MIRAÏ

www.miraifilm.co.uk

MIRAI
(Mirai no Mirai, 2018)

A four-year-old boy named Kun-chan is jealous of his newborn sister, who gets all the attention from his parents. Feeling deprived of his parents' love, he meets a mysterious girl named Mirai, who calls him Big Brother. This is the beginning of a great adventure for Kun-chan in settings where he encounters future or past versions of his relatives: his mother as a girl, his great-grandfather as a youngster, and his sister as a grown-up. Through all this, Kun-chan learns about the love of family.

MAKOTO SHINKAI (1973–)

Born in Nagano Prefecture, Japan in 1973, Makoto Shinkai made his commercial debut with the self-produced short film, *Voices of a Distant Star*. Since then, he has gone onto direct films such as *The Place Promised in Our Early Days* (2004), *5 Centimeters per Second* (2007), *Children Who Chase Lost Voices* (2011), and *The Garden of Words* (2013). In 2016, he directed *Your Name.*, an international sensation and social phenomenon in Japan. He quickly followed it up with *Weathering with You* in 2019, which set box office records in Japan. In November 2022, his latest film, *Suzume*, released in domestic movie theaters.

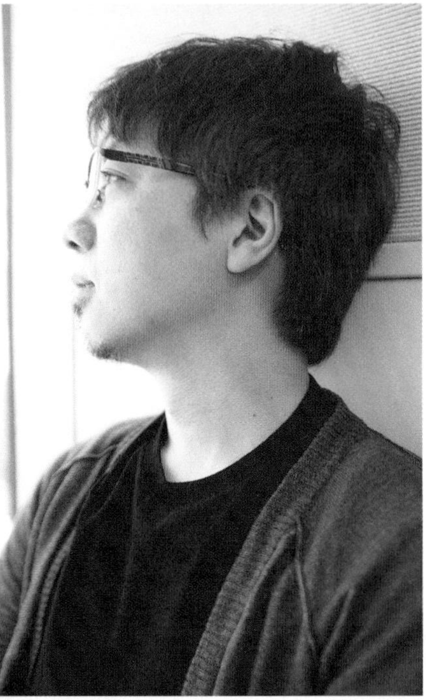

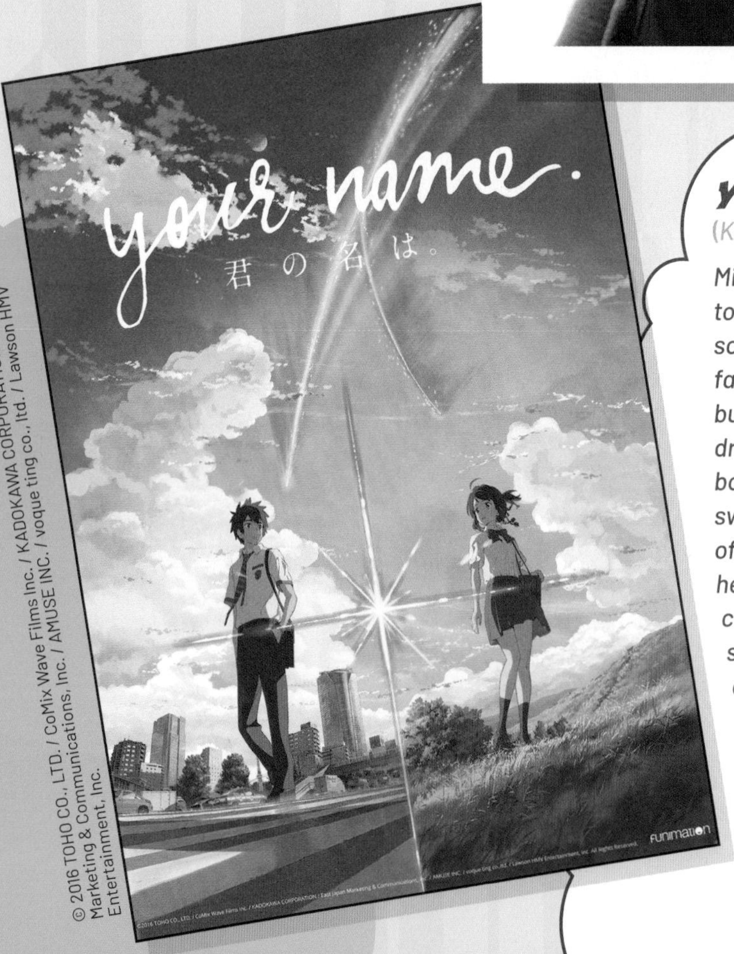
your name.
君の名は。
Funimation

YOUR NAME.

(Kimi no Na wa., 2016)

Mitsuha, a country girl who longs to live in Tokyo, and Taki, a high school student living with his father in Tokyo, have never met, but one day they realize in their dreams that they have switched bodies. Abruptly, however, the body switching stops. Taki goes in search of Mitsuha, relying on the scenery he saw in his dreams, but he is confronted with an unexpected scenario. Many viewers were drawn to Your Name.*'s overwhelming visual beauty and sentimental love story. The film was the highest-grossing film in Japan in 2016.*

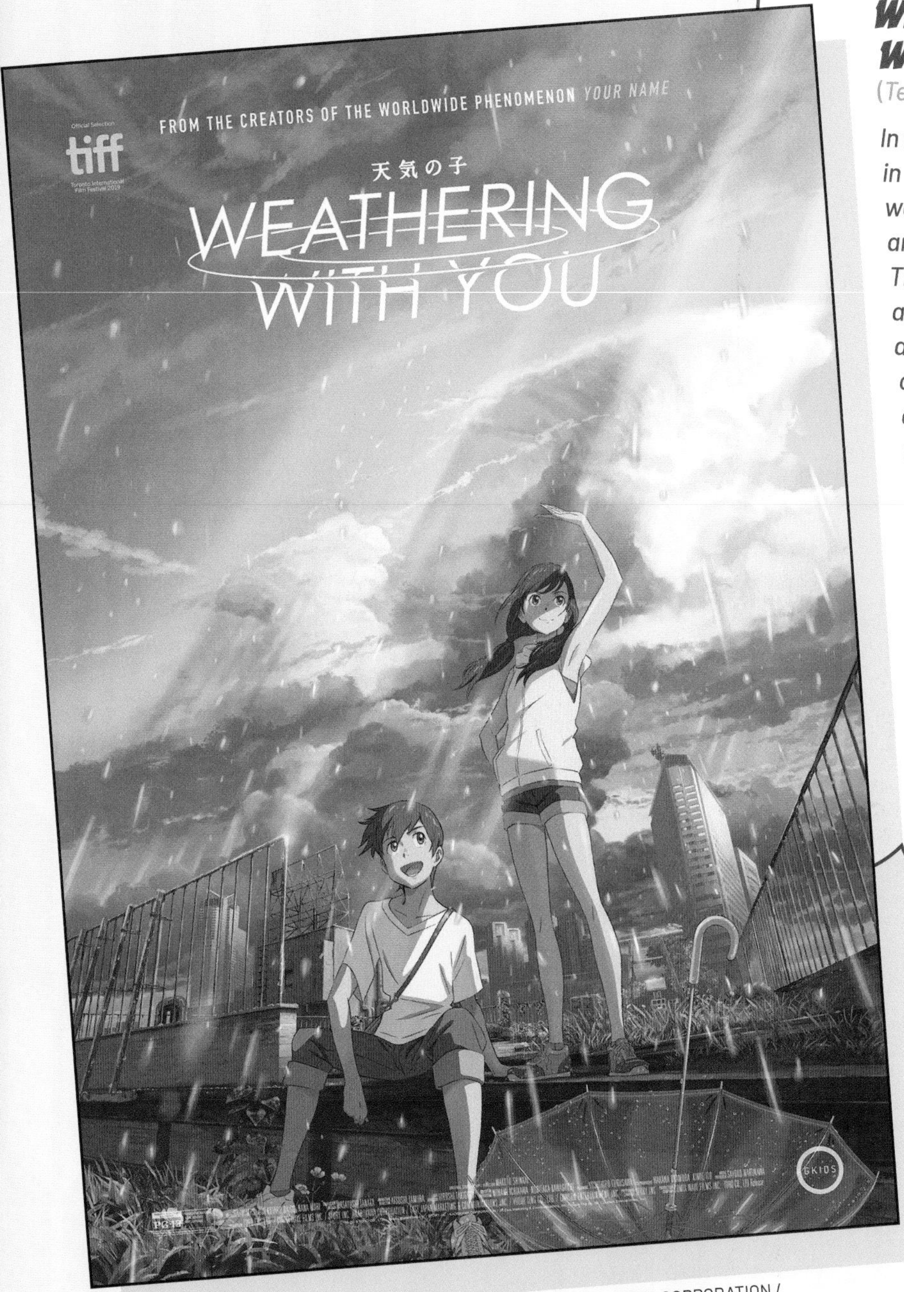
FROM THE CREATORS OF THE WORLDWIDE PHENOMENON YOUR NAME
tiff
天気の子
WEATHERING WITH YOU
GKIDS

© 2019 TOHO CO., LTD. / CoMix Wave Films Inc. / STORY inc. / KADOKAWA CORPORATION / JR East Marketing & Communications, Inc. / voque ting co., ltd. / Lawson Entertainment, Inc.

WEATHERING WITH YOU

(Tenki no Ko, 2019)

In this film set in Tokyo in the near future, the weather is abnormal and never stops raining. The plotline revolves around a runaway boy and a girl who can clear the rain clouds and let in the sun. This film is known for the outstanding quality of the animation of rain and the beautiful scenery of Tokyo. It debuted as the number one film at the Japanese box office in 2019.

NAOKO YAMADA (1984–)

In 2016, Naoko Yamada directed the blockbuster *A Silent Voice*, which won numerous film awards. A unique feature of Yamada's direction is her portrayal of emotions. Her works are known for their sensitive depiction of adolescents and their loneliness and vulnerability. In 2018, *Liz and the Blue Bird* (*Rizu to Aoi Tori*) was released, a story about the relationship between a high school oboe player and a flute player.

A SILENT VOICE
(*Koe no Katachi*, 2016)

This coming-of-age film by Naoko Yamada follows Shōko, a girl with a hearing and speaking impediment. While her classmates try getting along with her, one classmate, Shōya, torments her constantly. Later Shōya himself falls victim to bullying, while Shōko has transferred to another school. Time passes, and Shōya is now a high school student. He reunites with Shōko, looking to atone for his past behavior.

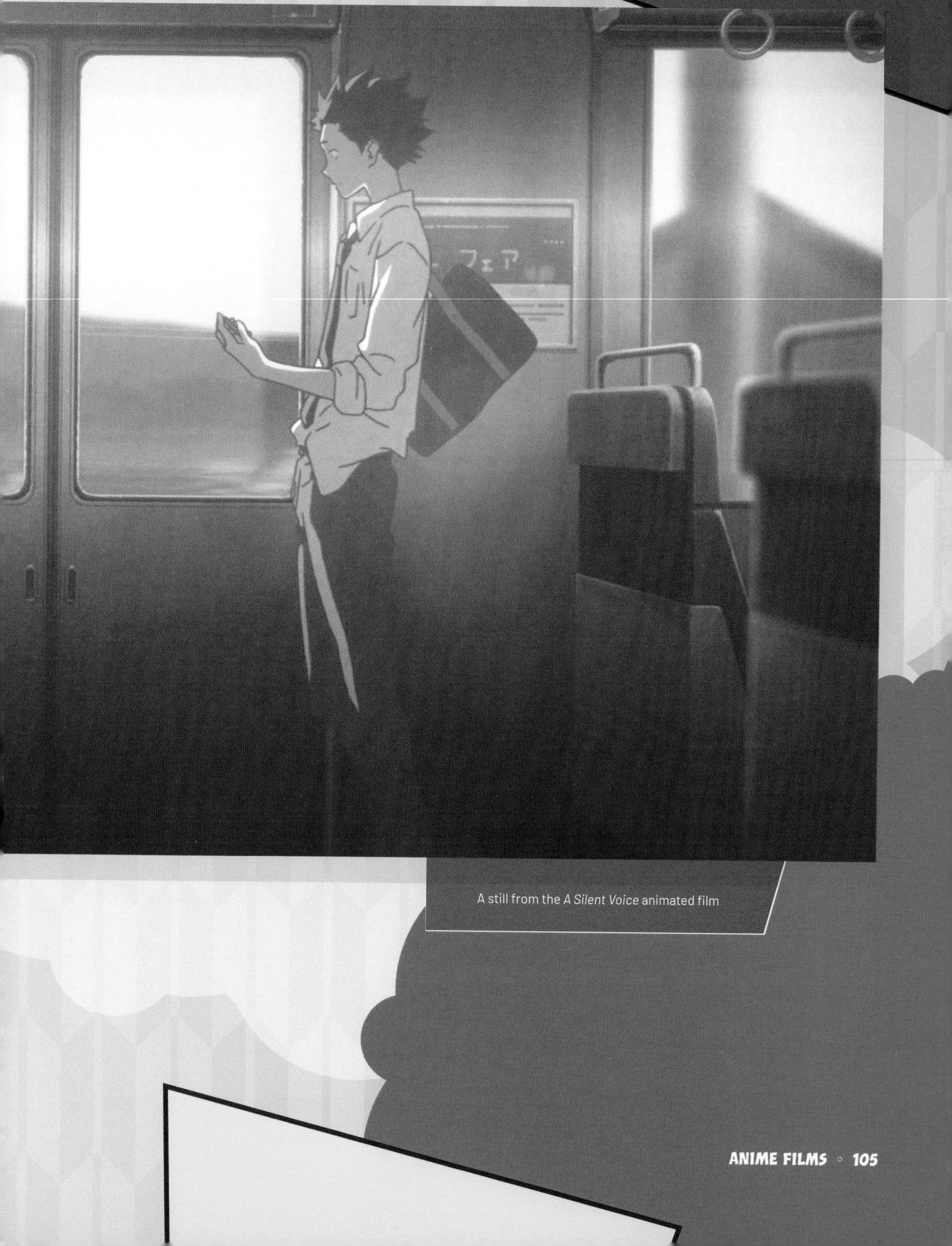
フェア

A still from the *A Silent Voice* animated film

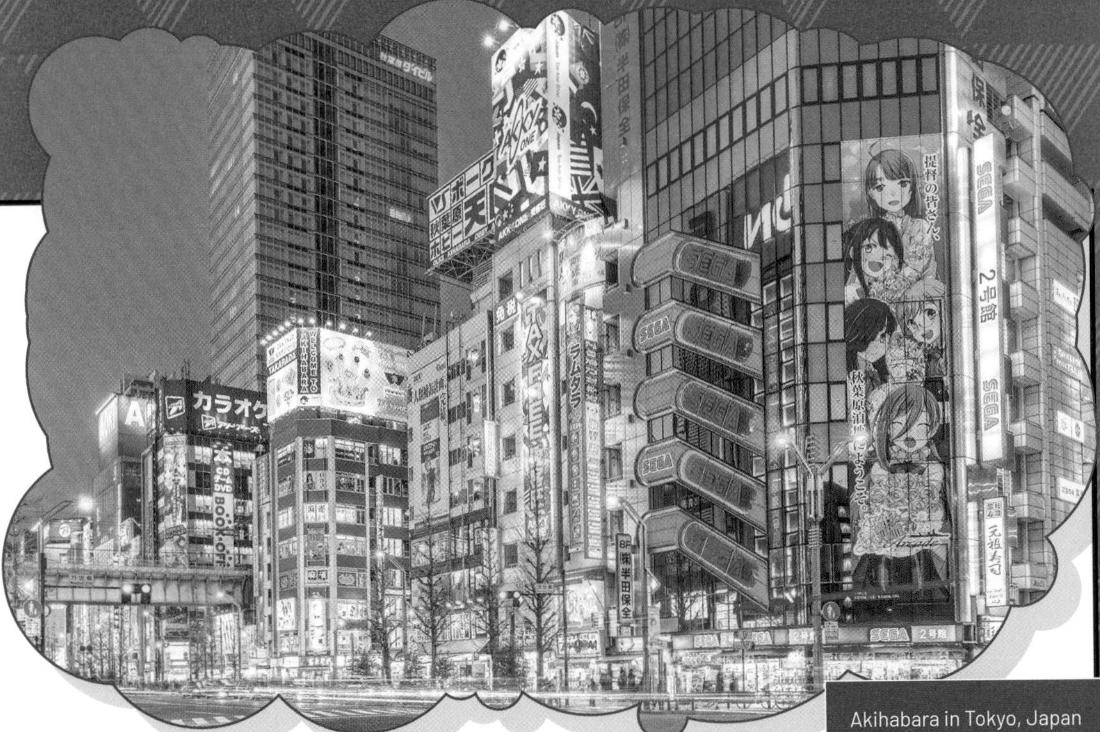
SEGA
カラオケ
BOOK·OFF
2号館
提督の皆さん、

Akihabara in Tokyo, Japan

OTAKU CULTURE

オタク文化

Have you ever heard of the term *otaku*? It originated in the early 1980s and describes a person deeply in love with their favorite things or areas of interest. In Japanese, the word *otaku* literally means *your home*, but is used in formal language in place of saying *you*. However, manga and anime enthusiasts used this term to refer to one another, and these people eventually became known as *otaku*.

The word *otaku* once conveyed a negative image, but that stigma faded. In the 2000s, the live-action movie *Train Man* (*Densha Otoko*, 2004) helped to positively redefine the image of *otaku* in the public's mind. It tells the story of a timid young *otaku* man who falls in love with a pretty woman after saving her from a drunk man on a train. He considers asking her out on a date, but lacking knowledge and experience, he seeks advice from others on an internet message board. As the story progresses, everyone roots for him to succeed in his pursuit of love. Thanks to this pure love story, the image of *otaku* transformed into a positive one of people devotedly pursuing their interests.

One entertaining aspect of the *otaku* culture is *dōjinshi*—booklets self-published by creators who want to show their enthusiasm for manga, anime, novels, or video games. Comiket (Comic Market), held in Tokyo, is the world's largest *dōjinshi* exhibition and an important social gathering where *otaku* share common interests. In the 1990s, the number of participants at Comiket exceeded 200,000—by 2019, that number climbed to 750,000.

As *otaku* culture has grown, it has attracted people who have never watched anime before. Various industries became interested in anime because *otaku* tend to spend a lot of money on the things they adore. As the *otaku* market keeps expanding, more companies want a piece of the action.

A prime example is *Mr. Osomatsu* (*Osomatsu-san*), a gag anime that depicts the daily lives of the adult sextuplet Matsuno brothers. It was produced in 2015 for the 80th anniversary of *manga-ka* Fujio Akatsuka's birthday and is a sequel to the original *Osomatsu-kun* series, in which the Matsuno brothers were children.

The six brothers, voiced by six popular male *seiyū* (voice actors), attracted many new fans, women especially. *Mr. Osomatsu* went beyond the boundaries of traditional anime because it organized partnerships with businesses like convenience stores and government offices. Magazines that displayed the characters on their covers sold out, and their DVDs were also in high demand. Some anime magazines estimate that in its first five months on the air, *Mr. Osomatsu* generated 7 billion yen for the Japanese economy, the equivalent of $51 million US!

DVDs, CDs, and marketing merchandise are a mainstay of the anime industry, but today's anime businesses increasingly look to sell services and experiences. Experiences and services like anime cafés, stage performances, and live concerts by *seiyū* are in great demand. At Universal Studios Japan, anime collaborations with *Detective Conan*, *Demon Slayer: Kimetsu no Yaiba*, and *Sailor Moon* created quite a buzz.

Attendees at Comiket

MOE

The term *moe* (mo-ey, moé) was first used as a slang word by Japanese anime fans. The original meaning is "young leaves sprouting," but in anime, it refers to something adorable, innocent, or cute, like big eyes and cat-ear headbands. The meaning of *moe* expanded to include cute girls and boys and their way of speaking, and now it has come to signify whatever one likes or finds exciting.

In 2008, the Akita Komachi rice producers introduced a special edition package printed with a *moe*-style cute girl designed by a famous illustrator. The company began accepting pre-orders online, but within five days, orders for this *moe* rice jumped to nearly five times the company's output of the previous year. They couldn't handle the onslaught and temporarily stopped taking orders! The campaign even captured the attention of consumers who had cut back on eating rice. Nowadays, beyond the food industry, all sorts of products and services—including textbooks, household items, tourism, and even police recruitment campaigns—have jumped on the *moe* bandwagon to boost sales or public interest.

COSPLAY

Cosplay is an English term created in Japan from the words "costume play" and refers to fans dressing up as characters from their favorite manga, anime, or video games. People who engage in cosplay are called cosplayers.

During the 1990s, fans of anime and manga began cosplaying. Since the 2000s, with the spread of the internet, it has become easier to obtain information on anime, manga, and cosplay. In this connected environment, the number of people cosplaying has risen dramatically. As Japanese anime has spread internationally, cosplay has caught on in other countries.

These days there are many related events, such as cosplay dance parties and cosplay photo shoots. The World Cosplay Summit, launched in Nagoya, Japan, in 2003, set a world record in 2022 as the longest-running cosplay-dedicated event.

ANIME CONVENTION

AnimeJapan is the world's largest anime event. Since 2014, it has been held annually and features over 200 anime-related companies and more than 150,000 visitors. In addition to numerous exhibition booths and product sales, the event also features *seiyū*, cosplay, and many other anime-related activities.

Anime events are held not only in Japan but also all over the world. Famous events include Anime Expo in Los Angeles; AnimeNYC in New York; Anime North in Toronto, Canada; and Japan Expo in Paris, France. It's impressive how *otaku* culture draws hundreds of thousands of fans to such events!

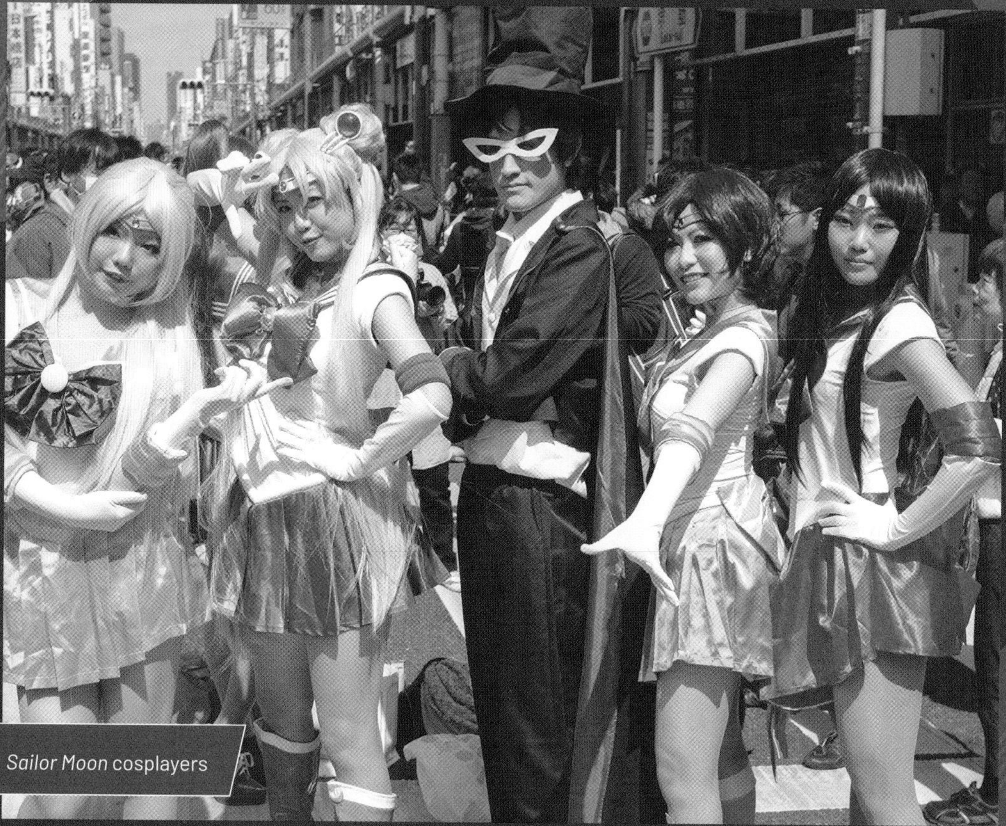

Sailor Moon cosplayers

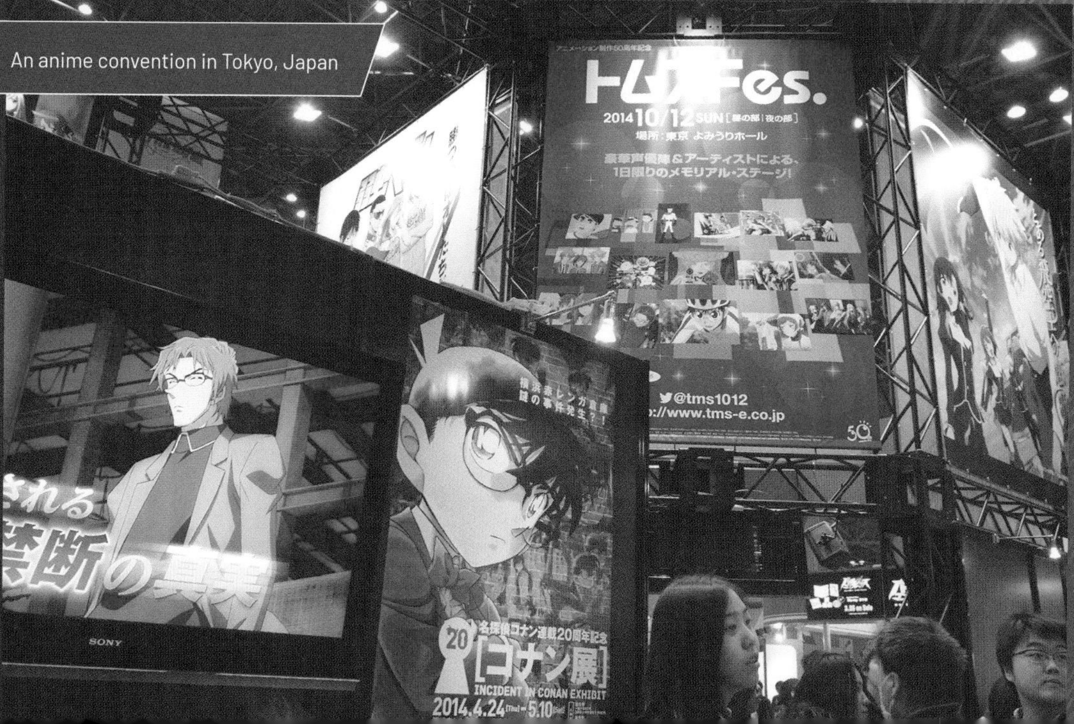

2014 10/12 SUN
場所：東京 よみうりホール
豪華声優陣＆アーティストによる、
1日限りのメモリアル・ステージ！
@tms1012
www.tms-e.co.jp
禁断の真実
SONY
名探偵コナン連載20周年記念
[コナン展]
INCIDENT IN CONAN EXHIBIT
2014.4.24

An anime convention in Tokyo, Japan

ANIME GOES GLOBAL
アニメの海外進出

ANIME COMMERCIALS

1 In recent years, a ton of Japanese TV commercials have been using anime to promote products. Anime presents an excellent potential for advertisers because it allows for a wide range of expression at significant cost savings since there is no need to hire actors. More and more *manga-ka* and anime directors are getting involved in making commercials for major companies as well. In 2022, anime film director Naoko Yamada created a commercial for Kit Kat. This short anime depicts the moment a young girl reads her mother's message on a Kit Kat wrapper, expressing her unspoken feelings.

Nausicaä of the Valley of the Wind kabuki, courtesy of Shochiku Co., Ltd.
© SHOCHIKU

ANIME KABUKI

The influence of Japanese manga and anime has reached the world of *kabuki*, a traditional Japanese performance art. These productions of anime- and manga-inspired *kabuki* are bringing in a new and younger fan base. At first glance, *kabuki* and manga/anime seem mismatched. However, manga and anime have well-defined character development that easily adapts to *kabuki*-style characters and concepts. The visual aspects of the characters—costumes, hairstyles, and makeup—in these new *kabuki* productions reveal a quality that manga/anime fans appreciate.

In 2015, *One Piece* was made into *kabuki*, followed by *Naruto* in 2018 and Hayao Miyazaki's *Nausicaä of the Valley of the Wind* in 2019.

ANIME EXPORTED ABROAD

When anime ship overseas, they often become subject to foreign countries' regulations. In the United States, for example, some violent scenes are not shown on television and the original animation undergoes other changes to reflect the country's customs.

Today *Dragon Ball Z* is immensely popular, but previously, many restrictions were placed on its US version. In some cases, entire episodes of the series were not shown due to the perception that it was too violent for young children. Despite this, *Dragon Ball Z* became a massive hit in 1998 when it debuted on Cartoon Network's Toonami television block with a version more closely representing the original Japanese version.

Changes are not made just because of violence, however. The 2014 US version of *Doraemon* is not set in Japan but in a fictional location in North America. Although the robotic cat's name remains Doraemon, the character Nobita is now called Noby, to help make it easier to remember for US audiences. Illustrations were also adjusted to reflect American culture and lifestyle— forks replaced chopsticks and dollar bills replaced Japanese money. Additionally, to promote healthy eating habits, scenes where Doraemon ate dessert were shortened and Nobita's snacks were changed to fruit.

Anime still from *Doraemon*, courtesy of Shin-Ei Animation Co., Ltd.

© Fujiko-Pro, Shogakukan, TV-Asahi, Shin-ei, and ADK

Another example of how anime is adapted and localized for a new environment is *Star of the Giants*. This famous baseball anime was remade into an Indian version called *Suraj the Rising Star* in 2012. The story's sport was changed from baseball to cricket to fit Indian customs. The story takes place in Mumbai, where Suraj, a young boy living in a slum, aspires to become a cricket star under the training of his strict father.

CAREERS IN ANIME
アニメ業界

Now that you've learned about the history of anime and its genres, let's take a look at some of the careers that people who help put it all together!

An animator is a person in charge of some part of an anime production process. There are three types of animators: key animators, in-between animators, and animation directors—their tasks differ significantly.

KEY ANIMATOR

The key animator draws the layout and keyframes, including characters and backgrounds, according to the storyboard (the graphic representation of how the anime will move from frame to frame). The key animator starts by meeting with the director and producer and then takes charge of placing the characters and shaping the anime's worldview. It is a job for those who love the creative process!

IN-BETWEEN ANIMATOR (INBETWEENER)

The inbetweener draws and connects the keyframes drawn by the key animator, so the anime flows naturally. This vital job directly affects how the anime characters' emotions and natural movements will appear on-screen.

ANIMATION DIRECTOR

The animation director's main task is to check the quality of each illustration drawn by the key animator and ensure there are no errors. If any illustrations are unacceptable, the animation director requests a correction. This very responsible position requires a combination of ability, experience, and a good eye!

Anime requires a high level of concentration and drawing skill. It is a job that attracts creative people who want to make a living doing what they love. If you are enthusiastic about honing your drawing skills and presenting your creativity to the world, consider becoming an animator in the future!

INTERVIEW
ANIMATOR MASAKO SAKANO

Masako Sakano is an animator with over 40 years of experience in the animation industry. Masako began as an assistant animator on *Great Mazinger*. She then became a key animator and assistant animator on *Mobile Suit Gundam* before eventually working on Topcraft's *Nausicaä of the Valley of the Wind*.

She worked for Studio Ghibli as a freelance animator for over two decades, contributing to classic anime films like *My Neighbor Totoro*, *Kiki's Delivery Service*, *Princess Mononoke*, and *Spirited Away*.

Masako currently lives in France, where she works on European animations like *Mia and the Migoo*, *Dofus – Book 1: Julith*, and *Wolfwalkers*.

AT WHAT AGE DID YOU REALIZE YOU WANTED TO PURSUE A CAREER IN ANIMATION?

When I was three years old, I watched a lot of animation and made up my mind early. But I was lazy and didn't study how to draw, nor did I draw a lot. I vaguely decided that when I grew up, I would be someone who creates cartoon movies.

WAS THERE A SPECIFIC ANIMATION OR ANIMATOR THAT IMPACTED YOU GREATLY AS A CHILD?

The Little Prince and the Eight-Headed Dragon, in which Mr. Yasuji Mori participated. Toei Animation's old feature films were often broadcast on TV at the time. Warner Bros. Animation's *Tom and Jerry* and Hanna-Barbera's TV series were also being shown daily, so they became everything in my life.

With the start of Japanese animation, my interest continued with *Astro Boy*, *Fujimaru of the Wind*, and *Hustle Punch*.

HOW LONG DOES IT TYPICALLY TAKE TO ANIMATE A SCENE?

It is quite different depending on the projects, scenes, and shots. In the case of key animation, it takes a day for simple works—around three to five shots or four to six seconds of animation. For more complex works, it can take a day for a half-second to two-second scene.

In the case of in-between animation, it takes 20 to 50 images per day for simple works and two to ten images for difficult work. For example, the scene in *Spirited Away* where Chihiro is in water was challenging, and it took two images a day.

IS THERE A CHARACTER YOU WORKED ON THAT YOU FEEL MOST CONNECTED TO?

That is difficult to answer. When you're working, you're absorbed in that character and become that character, but when you're done, you forget about it. That may be the secret to being able to do it for so long. (Laughs)

CAN YOU DESCRIBE YOUR FEELINGS WHEN YOU SEE A PROJECT YOU'VE WORKED ON PLAY AT A MOVIE THEATER OR A CHILD TAKING GREAT JOY IN A FILM OR ANIME YOU WORKED ON?

"Yes! Yatta! I made it!" I'm basically laughing in my head.

WHAT ADVICE WOULD YOU GIVE READERS INTERESTED IN PURSUING A CAREER IN ANIMATION?

If you want to be an animator, don't just watch Japanese animation; watch animations and movies from various countries. It is also important to move your body.

Movie still from *Spirited Away*

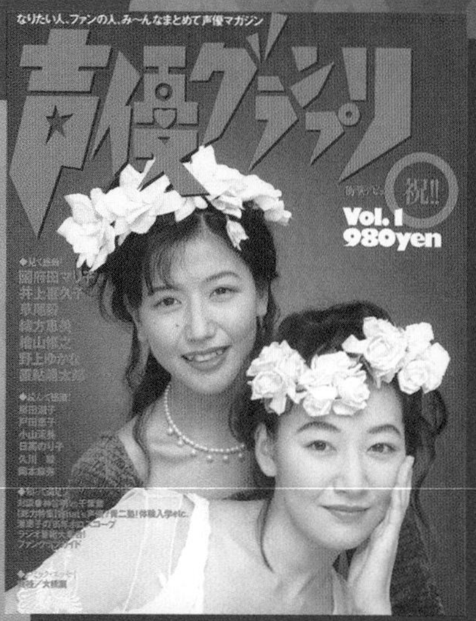
声優グランプリ
Vol. 1
980yen
Cover of the first volume of *Seiyū Grand Prix*

SEIYŪ

Seiyū (voice actor) is a popular profession in Japan. However, there was a time when voice acting was only a part-time job with a low salary. *Astro Boy*'s success led to new anime series, and TV anime became ever more popular, so the *seiyū* jobs attracted more attention. Due to the spread of anime in Japan, *seiyū* came to be recognized as a legitimate profession, not just a part-time job for actors.

The number of people aspiring to become *seiyū* is rising in Japan and it has become a highly competitive profession. There are schools and training sessions for voice actors, where students learn vocal exercises, emotional expression, reading, dubbing practice, and other skills needed to become *seiyū*.

There are several anime magazines in Japan, but also magazines dedicated to introducing the *seiyū* behind the characters. The first issue of *Seiyū Grand Prix* was published in 1994. It was the first monthly magazine to cover *seiyū* and information related to them, including concerts and events. The magazine also has features on *seiyū* schools for those who want to become voice actors, offering support to young readers who would like to pursue *seiyū* as their dream career.

It is also common for voice actor agencies to market *seiyū* for their full range of talents. For example, they can use their acting skills to work as stage actors, or if they are good singers, they can debut as singers.

The term *anison* (short for "anime song") refers to a wide variety of music, including theme songs and ending themes, as well as character songs in which the *seiyū* often sings. *Anison* got its start with *Astro Boy* in 1963.

In the 1970s, singers specializing in *anison* came into being and sang theme songs for many popular anime. In the 1980s, *anison* began to incorporate J-pop and built a new musical style; songs by J-pop singers unrelated to anime were often used as *anison*. The popularity of *seiyū* surged, and more and more *seiyū* sang theme songs for anime, which often reached the Top 10 on the music charts from the 1990s onward. In doing so, *anison* established itself as a crucial part of anime!

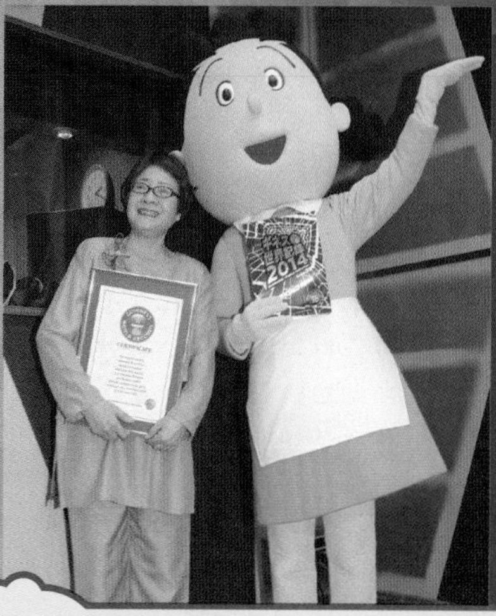

SO SUGOI!

Midori Kato, who has voiced the main character Sazae on *Sazae-san* since the beginning of the series in 1969, is recognized as having had the longest career as a voice actor vocalizing the same character in an animated TV series. *Sazae-san* has been on the air for over 50 years—*The Simpsons*, the longest-running animated US TV series, only began airing in 1989, so you can see how long-lived Sazae-san really is!

THE FUTURE OF MANGA AND ANIME

マンガとアニメのこれから

Part of the universal appeal of manga and anime is their characters. Through simplification and exaggeration techniques, protagonists are usually drawn without specific ethnic features. This makes it easier for people of different nationalities to identify with them. Foreign fans sometimes think they were created in their own country.

As visual media, manga and anime convey nonverbal messages through their images and are often enjoyed without dialogue. In anime, the soundtrack and sound effects engage viewers on an emotional level that transcends language.

CAN SOMEONE WITHOUT A QUIRK ...
...BECOME A HERO LIKE YOU?

Manga and anime have the power to fill viewers with positive energy, even saving them from despair and helping them overcome negativity. They often transmit uplifting messages such as "If you don't give up, you will accomplish good things" or "You can get along with people even when things are a little awkward." Most creators who produce manga and anime are not preaching but simply looking to please viewers and encourage good feelings. As a result,

Left: Panel from *My Hero Academia*, courtesy of VIZ Media
BOKU NO HERO ACADEMIA © 2014 by Kohei Horikoshi/SHUEISHA Inc.

Above: Anime still from *My Hero Academia*, courtesy of Toho Co. Ltd.
© K. Horikoshi / Shueisha, My Hero Academia Project

Japanese manga and anime can instill a sense of hope in audiences that transcends cultural and language barriers. In today's world, it's rare to find international content that so deeply stirs viewers' emotions.

The universality of manga and anime lets audiences share similar emotions. For those of you who are manga and anime fans, why not create a manga or anime club to connect and share your passion with others? For those interested in getting into manga and anime but don't know where to start, if you see someone reading a manga or wearing an anime T-shirt, say hi and ask them about it. Maybe they have a manga or anime group you can check out. After all, fans like you make manga and anime an enduring culture that brings dreams, hope, and harmony to the world—it's a worthy passion to pursue!

GLOSSARY
用語集

AKAHON: a type of *kusazōshi* that was intended for children, featuring a red cover; also, a cheap type of manga popular immediately after World War II

ANIME: Japanese animation shows or films

ANISON: short for "anime songs"; these refer to a wide range of music, including main themes, end songs, and character songs

AOHON: a type of *kusazōshi* that was intended for older readers; it featured a blue cover

CEL: short for "celluloid"; a transparent sheet on which illustrations are hand-drawn or hand-painted

COSPLAY: an abbreviation for "costume play," it refers to fans dressing up as characters from their favorite manga, anime, or video games

DŌJINSHI: a booklet self-published by creators who want to show their enthusiasm for manga and anime

EMAKIMONO: a narrative picture scroll

FUKIDASHI: speech balloons

FUROKU: extra gifts that come along with manga magazines

GEKIGA: translated as "dramatic pictures," Japanese comics intended for adult audiences

GŌKAN: several *kusazōshi* combined into one volume

HITO-KOMA MANGA: one-frame manga

JIDŌ MANGA: a category of manga intended for elementary school students

JOSEI MANGA: a category of manga intended for adult women

KAKKOII: cool, good-looking

KAMISHIBAI: a Japanese paper art form

KAMISHIBAI-YA: a *kamishibai* storyteller

KASHIHON-YA: a Japanese book rental store

KAWAII: cute

KIBYŌSHI: a type of *kusazōshi* that was intended for adults; it featured a yellow cover

KODOMO MANGA: a category of manga intended for small children

KŌKA-SEN: effect lines

KOWAI: scary

KUROHON: a type of *kusazōshi* that was intended for older readers; it featured a black cover

KUSAZŌSHI: illustrated picture books that were classified by genre according to the color of the cover

MANGA: Japanese comics that are usually printed but found digitally as well

MANGA-KA: manga creator

MOE: one's affectionate feeling toward manga and anime

OMOSHIROI: interesting, funny

ONOMATOPOEIA: words that mimic actual sounds or directly represent human emotions and objects

OTAKU: a Japanese expression translated to *your home*, but is also used to mean someone devoted to a particular interest

SEINEN MANGA: a category of manga intended for young adult males and adults

SEIYŪ: voice actors

SHŌJO MANGA: a category of manga intended for young girls

SHŌNEN MANGA: a category of manga intended for young boys

SUGOI: awesome

SUPOKON: a genre that focuses on the fighting spirit in sports

UKIYO-E: a style of Japanese woodblock print

YŌKAI: supernatural beings and folktale creatures

YON-KOMA MANGA: four-frame manga

AFTERWORD
あとがき

As a teenager living in Osaka, Japan, manga and anime transported me from everyday life to a world of unbounded imagination. In my imaginary world, I would travel back several years in a time machine to talk to my younger self or set off on adventures to uncover lost treasures. There were so many manga I wanted to read to expand my imagination, but I didn't have the money to buy manga magazines every week. At that time in Japan, many people read manga magazines on the train and, once done, would leave them on the bench at the station or on the train. Reading magazines on my way home from school that someone had left behind became a cherished hobby. Eventually, I illustrated my own manga, intending to become a *manga-ka* (manga artist) and realize the dream of drawing like the legendary Fujiko • F • Fujio.

After graduating from high school, I got busy with college and work, and a large part of my life was spent dealing with new passions, such as studying English and socializing with new friends, so I had less time to spend on my love of manga and anime. But then, after more than 25 years, I had the opportunity to work as an educator in the United States and teach manga and anime history at a university. Many of my students knew more about the subject than I did, so I started exploring these media again, following their recommendations. As a result, the excitement of my childhood days returned.

You never know what adventures life will bring. When I was a teenager, I never dreamed I would one day teach Japanese language and culture in New York City at Columbia University and New York University. I never imagined that the knowledge of manga and anime I gained as a teenager would become part of my future career and allow me to share my passion through this book you hold in your hands.

May your passions lead you to a beautiful future.

—SHUICHIRO TAKEDA

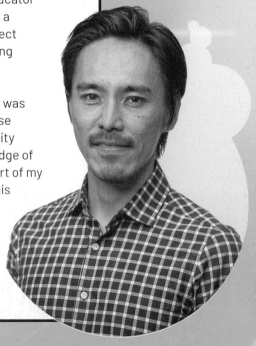